Blog off in a B and

Campervan Travels around the British Coast

By Pat Heaven

Dedicated to

Past, present and future family and friends.

Also all sea lovers.

"The sea once it casts its spell, holds one inside its nets of wonder forever"

Jacques Yves Cousteau

Table of Contents

Introduction

"Travelling leaves you speechless then turns you into a storyteller. "

Ibn Battuta

This is why I have a story to tell.

I always thought I had some gypsy blood in me and, given the opportunity, I would bring to life the dream that I had held onto since I was 18 years old. This was to travel around the whole coast of Britain in a campervan.

I finished my work in the NHS, probably before I should have, took my money and ran. I saw this trip as no big deal really, just an ordinary simple travelling life with a difference. Apart from experiencing the Snowdon Zipwire (which was pretty exciting) the day before my departure there were no extreme sports involved, but my biggest and most exciting challenge

1

was to endure the Scottish Highlands in winter, without heating. I must admit that occasionally I became obsessed with going down every track so at times I had to restrain myself. However, I can now proudly say that I must have travelled along most of the small coastal roads that hug the British Coast.

Before my travels most people's reactions were positive, but a few disapproved of my plans. It is not the done thing to leave your "other half" on his own for a year and a half. A bit rich as K was a full grown man of 57 years. Other people were astonished that I was travelling on my own. When I said I was looking forward to camping in forests etc., they were shocked that I was not scared of "being axed in the woods by a psycho". I mean, there was more chance of me being stabbed before I left south east London!

My aspirations for writing this book are to share my experience of the journey and inform the reader of all the varied and beautiful remote beaches and villages of the British coast. I kept a daily diary as I went along which I edited into a notebook every few days. On my return to London I redrafted this, so not every place I visited or stayed is included in this text. However, you can see photos of most of the places I visited set out in monthly albums if you send an email to me at **blogoff@f2s.com**; I will respond with a link to Flickr.

This book has been written in a very casual way in the hope that it may portray a sense of actually travelling with me. Any unfamiliar phrases, words or abbreviations can be found in the key at the back of the book.

A small disclaimer now:

Any historical or geological fact may well be inaccurate as I only wish to show an overview compared to detailed information that you can acquire on Google. Nonetheless, with the same tool, you can view most of the places covered in this book. It is a sad fact now that there are few secret places left due to Google, but the advantage is that places can be shared and hopefully respected. I feel very strongly that people when wild camping leave the places as they found them. If too many vans park up together, it cannot only spoil the place but can also be intimidating to the locals. This is why I generally parked up in secluded areas away from big groups of vans.

However, I feel passionately that people, especially women, should follow their dream, in their own way, whatever that may be, undeterred by superfluous external pressures.

Preparation

I fell in love with my Mazda Bongo the day I saw it online. The male seller had not even bothered to wash it, and it was blatantly obvious that it had to go: the wife hated it!

Once washed, it looked so smart, all painted black with tinted windows. It was a little too serious actually. It looked like a cross between a London gangster van and private ambulance. "Hippie Stickers" were the answer. A few stars on the roof, Celtic symbol on the bonnet, Banksy girl and balloon on one side and three elephants on the other made it look more playful. A pentangle on the back gave it a bit of an edge and all the stickers were in gold. I was pleased with the result and I still think that it looks quite classy.

I kitted it out with everything I needed for the journey. To maximise space things ideally had to have two purposes and I bought a new range of collapsible items. This included a kettle, sieve, toast rack, toaster, bucket and dog bowl. The van had a JAL side conversion which meant that the dual hob and sink was opposite the sliding door. Underneath, next to the fridge, a small cupboard housed the plates and cutlery. Everything else fitted into the remaining limited cupboard space and four boxes stacked behind the back seat. These boxes were for food, pans and books. Stored under the bed were the spare gas cylinder, "bucket" BBQ, windbreak and emergency trowel. This tool was only used on about six occasions when no public convenience or pub was available! My cut down wellies and shoes were stored in a flexible bucket by the cupboard behind the driver's seat out of the way. As the van had no wardrobe I kept all my clothes in a small suitcase on the passenger seat. Toiletries fitted conveniently in the space where there had originally been a tiny Japanese video TV. The back of the van stored the table and chairs, only used when I had visitors on very sunny days, and the sleeping bag and pillow went in the tall cupboard. Most of the time I slept "downstairs" in the rock and roll bed, but on campsites I would sleep "upstairs" on my lilo in the mushroom roof. The roof is raised manually using an adapted yacht pole. There was a place for everything and everything in its place. This allowed me to keep my three-foot lounge tidy and gave the illusion of space in the van. I placed blue webbed matting on the lounge floor. Not only was this warm but also functional as all the sand and dirt conveniently fell through the holes.

The van was to be my home for nearly a year and a half so I wanted to give it a feminine touch. Homemade painted gypsy mirrors hung down from the ceiling, curtains separated the living section from the driver's seat and mushroom stickers decorated bare surfaces. Colourful bunting adorned the dash and windows and coloured LED lighting gave it the warm ambiance that I desired. Incidentally, I named her Billie!

Man Facts

Campervan type	Mazda Bongo 2 litre engine, fitted with solar panel on the roof
Total mileage	13,272 miles
Bongo repairs	MOT, brakes, steering, leisure battery and fan belt costing approx. £1,000
Petrol expenses	£3,080
Oil top ups	7 times
Photos taken	4,053 to be edited
Ferry expenses	£400
Gadgets	Brian my Samsung tablet, Courtney my personal mobile Wi-Fi, Winston my music Beats Pill and Ben my basic mobile phone.
Tools	Saw, hammer, pliers, screwdrivers and a constant supply of Gaffer tape
Budget	£200 per week including petrol
Fun money	Lots above my initial budget
On the road	560 days

Planning and My String Theory

I planned to start my journey in March 2014 and decided that 18 months would be a good amount of time to be on the road. This meant two summers and one winter in the van. Crowded school holidays around Devon were unavoidable, as was winter in Scotland as I was starting my trip from North Wales. To break the journey down into months, I developed my own string theory. This consisted of placing a piece of string around a map of the British coast and dividing into eighteen, one section for every month. Therefore, give or take 50-100 miles, I could keep on my own track, but be free to go where I wanted when I wanted. Nowhere on the journey was pre-planned or booked in advance, apart from meeting up with people along the way. I wanted to rely on local people to guide me. This worked great sometimes, but was tricky other times when locals only knew a few miles down the road. My sense of direction is quite honestly abominable, but luckily my map reading skills are good. I travelled anticlockwise and as long as the sea was on my right I knew I was going the correct way.

Why did I start my journey from Portmeirion? Simply because it is my favourite place, thanks to its stunning setting and amazing architecture. The village was built by Sir Clough Williams-Ellis between 1925 and 1975 in order to pay tribute to the Mediterranean atmosphere. It certainly does that and I am not alone in my admiration for the place. It has been the location for numerous music videos, film sets and the well known 1977 TV series "The Prisoner".

It was a wonderful feeling to leave the village, turn right and know that I would return eventually from the other side having gone full circle around Britain.

I did join some helpful organisations: The Camping & Caravanning Club, Bongo Fury, Brit Stops and the National Trust. The last of these was invaluable for free parking as I was doing the trip within an allocated weekly budget. In reality, it was hard to stick within it due to various unforeseeable expenses and my belief that I needed to spend a bit more during the trip to maximise my fun. Despite this, my whole eighteen-month trip cost less than your average three-week cruise, which for me puts it all in perspective and leaves me feeling quite smug.

My priority was to stay in out-of-the-way places only passing through big towns and cities when I had to. I only went on the motorway once, around Bristol; otherwise, I took the smallest roads that I could find that hugged the coast. The majority of the time I wild camped (or rough parking as I called it) but when in need of a shower or laundry I would stay at a basic and cheap campsite, Youth Hostel, bunkhouse or bothy. Very occasionally, when friends visited I stayed in a B&B and as a treat, a hotel paid for by K. My preference was to wild camp in remote areas such as RSPB or NT places, moor land, headlands, lighthouses or forests. The ultimate priority was to have a sea view and whenever possible I would park the van so that the sliding door was facing the sea. This way I could pull up

the blind in a morning, admire the seascape and sip my
tea whilst still in bed.

Incommunicado

K and my daughter insisted that I take a mobile phone for emergencies. I had refused to own one prior to this but considered it a reasonable request and agreed. My part of the deal was to only have it switched on for two hours one night of the week. This was the only phone connection to my "other life" and worked out fine as a lot of the time I was travelling without a signal anyway.

I also had Brian, my newly acquired tablet that could speak to Courtney my personal Wi-Fi and hence keep in touch with people via email, which I found less intrusive. I had many a giggle at my friend Anje's long reports of her latest conquests with her various internet dating subjects whereas snail mail was used to keep in touch with my Luddite friend Kit in Portugal. Her return letters were delivered via motorbike courier, courtesy of K on his visits to see me. Granddaughters Lola and Dot also received intermittent jolly postcards from all around the coast. My only entertainment was reading "recycled" books and music from Brian played through Winston. I also had a Kindle, mainly used to look up Jon Gunter's invaluable book about his similar trip a few years ago. My "Wild Swimming COAST" book was a present for my trip, and it became almost like my personal bible for finding magical swims, out of the way beaches and coves.

Some people suggested that I write a daily blog - hence the name of this book. I was really quite horrified at this idea, as I wanted to live my travelling life without reporting it to anyone at the time. This may seem weird in this age of social media, but for me, a simple existence for a year and a half sounded absolute bliss.

For company I had my 12-year-old springador dog called Loki (lord of mayhem and mischief). She is not the brightest dog on the planet but is good natured, well balanced and self-contained: an ideal travel companion. She was a useless guard dog and did not say much, but her companionship was invaluable. Over the months, she changed from a fat London dog to a lithe chilled out creature. She would excitedly jump out of the van straight up the coastal path, or sprawl out on the pub floor as relaxed as if she was at home. People would fall in love with her, but she would tend to ignore their attention as if to say, "I'm a dog, get on with it!"

The Journey Begins
March 22nd 2014 – Portmeirion to Llangrannog

"The woman who follows the crowd will usually get no further than the crowd and the woman who walks alone is likely to find herself in places no-one has ever been"

Albert Einstein

It was a grey day on Saturday 22nd March 2014 when I left the comfort of a warm cottage in the village of Portmeirion. I turned right on the main road contemplating what "roughing it" for eighteen months would feel like.

Driving south, the weather got darker and darker until I reached Harlech, which is where I dropped off K to catch his bus back to London. There were no tears, just hugs and kisses as we parted in a howling wind and barrage of hailstones. It was a memorable start to my journey. What had I let myself in for? Trepidation enveloped me, but soon my excitement took over and I carried on regardless, with my bag of mixed feelings and Loki curious as to where we were going.

The weather soon cleared so I put up the Bongo roof in what I considered a sheltered spot on the campsite at Llanbedr, Shell Island. Later in the night, the wind got right up and the roof was swaying badly, so at 6am. I panicked and got up to close it, but before I could, it closed itself on top of my head! That was the first night, one I will not forget in a hurry. I left the following morning taking away with me sound advice from a fellow traveller who had stayed in the Outer Hebrides in January. He told me to get some pure silk pyjamas to keep warm. I liked his style.

Passing through Barmouth, and winding my way inland around the first of the many estuaries near Dollgelau and sleepy Fairbourne, I reached Tonfanau which was my first "rough parking" (wild camping) night in the middle of nowhere. It was quite eerie; there is only a tiny unmanned station and disused air base camp with derelict buildings and gunneries. I felt quite spooked by the strange noises in the night, which actually turned out to be the fridge switching itself off and on.

It may seem that I actually rushed around Wales, as I only stayed a total of 31 days. This was because I have lived in Wales for many years and was already familiar with numerous beautiful coastal places, so I tended to visit towns and beaches as opposed to staying the night. I had itchy feet to reach unfamiliar places and be surprised.

Aberdyfi is an unspoilt and pleasant Victorian seaside town and Ynyslas a great expanse of sand and dunes next to the small linear town of Borth. The beach at Ynyslas holds fond memories for me as it was where I first drove my dad's car, sat on several cushions to see over the windscreen aged nine. Of course I got stuck in the sand and got told off for it!

Next, I stayed two nights with a friend, Elaine, who lives in Aberystwyth, but I did park along the front by the castle along with other campervans. I did not realise until then what a competitive and male domain I had entered: size matters and all that. I met a bolshie man who parked in a massive converted coach next to me. He kept boasting about his huge space, wood burners and gadgets. I much preferred the younger couple, Dave and Jenny from Yorkshire, who humbly showed me their scruffy £700 VW conversion complete with disguised port-a-loo, which doubled as a dining table.

Then I did my first stupid thing: I left the tailgate of the van open for two hours whilst I had breakfast with Elaine. Walking back over the castle to the van my face was a picture of horror. Fortunately nothing was stolen so all was well. It restored my faith in human nature.

Passing through Aberaeron I stopped at Newquay to see if there were any dolphins swimming in the harbour as I have seen them there many times before. No luck this time, but I walked along the lovely stone jetty in the sunshine with the boats bobbing up and down in the harbour accompanied by the usual smells of fish. A personal calamity occurred on the way to Llangrannog. Being a good female mechanic, I stopped at a garage to check the tyre pressures and then went for a wee. There was no light and someone (probably a woman) had put the toilet seat lid down. Result... wet clothes from the bottom down! However, I soon sorted myself out by finding a stream to sit in and the wind dried me off.

Whilst having a drink in the pub in Llangrannog, the proprietor told me about a man, Christian Knott, who was walking around Britain for charity. I think he was trying to make me feel uncharitable, but it did not work.

The next day I tried to find a "wild swimming" beach, but the rope ladder down the cliff had been removed, so I did not make it. I also discovered that where I had parked for the night was next to a sewer manhole. In the morning a chap woke me up emptying it. He was whistling while he worked so very happy and chatty, talking to me about the weather. He also confirmed that it was fine for me to stay the night there providing I did not block his hole! Later on I watched a Remembrance service near the very large steep sided rock on the beach. The mourners were all very young and I wondered if a youngster had fallen from that rock on to the beach. It seemed inappropriate to ask so I will never know. Petals were being thrown everywhere; it was all very moving. Then a big group of "Didcot Phoenix" cyclists arrived. I was unsure if it was designer label or a club, but seeing so many men swaddled in Lycra, sent me on my way double quick!

That evening, I had my first toddler sit on the Bongo step. He had taken a shine to Loki. When I asked him his name, he said "free" but that was really Michael's age.

April 2014 - Mwnt to Porlock

> "Not all that glitters is gold, not all those who wander are lost "
>
> **JRR Tolkien**

At Mwnt, I stayed at a lovely farm and was woken up by the cows and a very strong smell of manure. I saw Griff Rhys Jones on the cliffs with his film crew. He was well chumpy and did not say hello when I nodded to him. He was just stomping around the place looking quite pissed off. I admire his passion for Wales, but much preferred him when he was funny and jolly in his previous comic role in the well-known TV series "Not The Nine O'clock News".

Further on, Cardigan Castle was shut, but a woman told me that I had not missed much as there was only "a muddy field and a few trees inside". A builder there informed me that they were spending £10 million restoring it, so I told him he had better make a good job of it.

My first "Brit Stop" pub was the Salutation Inn at Felindre Farchog. The landlady set the dinner table for two, and it made her laugh when I told her that the dog had already eaten. I had a mental picture of Loki looking lovingly into my eyes across the dinner table whilst eating a sausage!

The next night was spent at Porthgain next to an award winning fish restaurant. I had had a great day swimming in the Blue Lagoon, a disused quarry with wonderful turquoise water at nearby Abereiddy.

The next day I travelled through the port of Fishguard and on to St. Davids with its magnificent cathedral and eventually arrived at Whitesands Bay, where I saw my first porpoise of the trip and mixed with the surfers. One of them said something of mine was awesome (or was it awful?), but I am not quite sure what. They spend most of their time watching waves and practising on a funny contraption. This is a reel with a board on top and they practice balancing by gyrating their hips. It is most enjoyable to watch, especially if you have nothing better to do. I also spotted numerous surfers hiding from the cold wind donned with black wetsuits, looking to me like a cross between a frog and a pelican.

A quick stop at lovely Solva with its tiny harbour was where I replenished my water supply and did a small local shop. Unbeknown to me at the time, the village was recently used as part of the location for the film Dylan Thomas's "Under Milk Wood". Newgale lived up to its name as usual. I camped in a quarry overlooking the bay; however, the view was invisible due to thick fog and relentless rain. It was here that I really felt I had left my old life behind. I was very amused by Loki the following morning, as her bum was too big for the space under the bed. She tried to get out from under the bed and got stuck which was very amusing. Who said a dog could not look embarrassed. The van also became trapped in the mud and we had to be pulled out by the farmer's tractor. The only other thing that happened at Newgale while Bongo bound (this means a rainy day spent inside) was that I managed to set my glasses on fire from the hob. This turned out to be an asset as the burnt knobbly bits made my glasses more secure on my head!

I walked through the Bosherton Lakes to the delightful beach of Broadhaven but Angle was my next stopover. The village overlooks the oil refinery but is quite a peaceful place. I stayed on a homely farm and helped bottle-feed the lambs. At the pub Loki hoovered up all the local football club's chips off the floor much to the delight of the owner. Unfortunately, the other very old 16th century village pub The Point House was closed.

Freshwater West was full of Bristol University engineer students all working hard which made me feel quite smug. The beach was littered with plastic debris and I met a couple of beach cleaners, they had found stuff from all over the world: an octopus net from California, a lobster cage from Mexico, and gun cartridges from Canada to name a few. Surprisingly they thought that the worst offenders for littering the sea are fishermen with their broken plastic nets and empty sandwich boxes. I stopped at Skrinkle Haven to walk to the gigantic rock formation known as the Church Doors. They are really quite impressive.

Going to the loo in the museum at Tenby, I voted it one of the nicest attic toilets in the UK due to its location on the rocky outcrop overlooking the sea. I then moved on to Saundersfoot, a lively little place where I came across a Dale Bowen art preview - champagne was flowing, so I had a glass (and an egg sandwich.) Good art work too.

At Pendine I watched men sand-surf on the massive speed-racing beach and bought some new colourful bunting for the dashboard as mine was beginning to look very tired.

Laugharne claims to have inspired the writer and poet Dylan Thomas. You can visit the boathouse where he lived, the shed where he wrote "Under Milkwood" and even the pub where he used to get paralytic on booze.

At Carmarthen, I felt a bit stressed due to the weight of traffic. I got my first angry beep from a man in a posh sports car. I thought it quite funny as I am so high up in the Bongo and he just looked small and quite insignificant down there.

Three Cliff's Bay is one of the best campsites in Wales with panoramic views overlooking the magnificent huge sandy bay and headlands of rocky outcrops. A "Mum and Dad" type couple run the site and are lovely, they work very hard to keep the place in pristine condition. You have to get there early in the day to secure a pitch on the wonderful cliff edge. Wild garlic was growing rampant, in the nearby valley, so I picked some and used it to cook a delicious Indian Aloo Gobi meal.

Further along the Gower peninsular, at Llanmadoc I shared a field/car park for the night with just lambs, sheep and wild horses wandering around. It was at the end of the road so lovely and quiet apart from the animal noises which I did not mind.

The next night, I was lording it with K at the King Head Hotel at Llangennith, luxuriating in the high bath and comfy bed. We also had an amazing swim on the beach in the Blue Pool, as it is known locally. The water really was turquoise in this impressive rock pool.

I drove through the Mumbles and outskirts of Swansea before stopping at Llantwit Major. The beach there is like a giant pool table with huge round boulders strewn across the chequered flat rock expanse. After Swansea, I was getting a bit stressed out with getting lost, so I chickened out and bought a Sat Nav. Just before K left me again, I nearly reversed over him on his motorbike, parked behind the Bongo. He was not amused, but two blokes looking on from a neighbouring van were in fits of laughter.

I was very anxious about driving on the motorway to get around Bristol and I could not get on with my new Sat Nav, so I had to do it the old-fashioned way with maps and written directions. I managed by following a very slow Argos van, eventually crossing the blustery Severn Bridge and made it into England.

Arrival in England

I followed the Severn estuary towards Weston-Super-Mare and parked up for the night at the end of a small dead end lane in Sand Point car park. It was my first big mistake and one that I would not repeat. I had just got soaked in a hailstorm walking on top of the moor, so I dried out inside and had an early night. I had just got to sleep when boy racers awakened me together with many young courting couples. Keeping a low profile I tried to ignore them, but then the flashing lights and horns started. Much to my relief, at about 10.30pm, they all disappeared. However, twenty minutes later a couple of burly blokes in a big white van arrived and they were definitely not lovers! I got in a bit of a panic, as by this time the windows were covered in condensation. It was time to move on, and sharpish. I got out of bed and then the van, at the same time as shouting to Loki "You're not getting out then?" and drove off. I did not fancy tackling two blokes with a crowbar on my own. My guess was that the youngsters had told them about the van, which they had assumed was empty, and the men that came later had come to break in. This was my one and only dodgy moment of the trip and a lesson well learned. It had not felt right and I should have moved earlier. They did not follow me and I parked up safely in a nearby lay-by next to some woods a few miles down the road. So gladly the episode all ended well.

I did not stop at Western–Super-Mare as I wished to get on, but took a photo of the very sad dilapidated pier.

Further on at Watchet, I went to look at several impressive huge snail shaped fossils on the beach. I liked the town and the people at Pebbles, the nearby Camra Bar of the Year, were very friendly. I spent a great evening there listening to a live band and chatting with the locals. One lady, Dizzy, insisted on showing me pictures on her phone of not only her children and dog, but donkey too!

The following day, rain at Blue Anchor was torrential, but this did not stop the 50 man fishing competition. They set themselves up about three hours before the tide arrives, even in the wind and rain. Unfortunately, Loki had gulped down a rancid fish, which reappeared a little later, luckily, not on the floor of the Bongo.

In Minehead, I stayed at a "mum and dad" C&C type campsite, with great views overlooking the town. I cannot fault these sites as they are always immaculately clean and the staff are polite and helpful, but everything seems so regimented there, it feels like staying at your parents as teenagers. Too well looked after for me! They have wardens on duty twenty four hours. Paul, the night warden, helpfully made me a list of campsites and places he thought I might like, further down the coast.

"What a lovely place to break down," was what the AA man said to me the following morning, as he recharged my battery. I had left the ignition on all night and so from then on I pulled the electric blinds down manually. I always thought that electronic blinds were a bit over the top anyway. On the road again, I visited Selworthy, a picture postcard village with wall-to-wall thatched cottages. I had a bit of a "discussion" in the National Trust shop about the jam I bought. I was trying to persuade the woman in the shop that what she called Whortles are really called Whimberries and she was not having any of it. In fact depending where you come from they can also called Billberries, Blaeberries, Myrtle blueberries or even Fraughans. Whatever, they are delicious.

May 2014 – Lynton to Watergate Bay

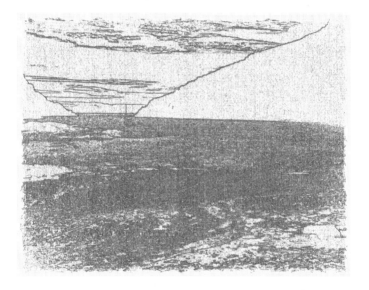

"I never travel without my diary. One should always have something sensational to read"

Oscar Wilde

Wandering down the village street at Porlock, I was referred to as "ma'am"! It made me feel half officially old, and half "Lady of the Manor" which I preferred. The museum also informed me of how in the 15th Century, people would hang their clothes in the garderobe (toilet) to get them smelly. This would supposedly stave off the rats!

At the camping site at Lynmouth, our neighbours in a "big white fridge" had two designer cats on leads outside. Loki seemed unperturbed by them as she was too busy munching a bone which I had bought from a proper butchers. Butchers to me always seem friendly, even if you tell them you are vegetarian but your dog is not. I think this must be due to all that intense chopping of bones that gets rid of all their aggression.

Behind Lynmouth on my moorland walk, I came across a man called Martin in an isolated spot on Holdstone Down. He looked as if he wanted to be on his own so I kept my distance, but we did get chatting. He was in remission for cancer and I was able to identify with him as I had been diagnosed and been through that same journey several years back. We talked about the way a cancer diagnosis radically changes your values and more positively how beautiful the scenery was. I hope he gets the all clear soon too! He informed me that the nearby Hangman's Point is the highest cliff in the UK. There are certainly 360° views around.

Near Broadhaven, I went down two hundred and forty steps in search of a "wild swimming" place, only to be disappointed as there were about twenty people all rigged up with wetsuits already swimming there. They were part of the North Devon Wild Swimming Club and I was invited to join their club. Well, I may seem ungrateful but my idea of a "wild swim" is to go swimming on your own, at a deserted spot, not, in a huge bunch to a crowded place in a wetsuit. Theirs is tame swimming to me, but I did not let my opinions be known. They thought I was a bit strange as I only had my swimming gear on and no wetsuit.

As I found out later, I had stayed the night near the famous artist Damien Hurst's mother's house. One dog walker in the woods admired my van and said I must go and see the Hurst sculpture of a pregnant woman "Verity" down by the harbour. It is striking, but not sure I particularly liked it.

In Ilfracombe, I paid my money and went for a swim in the Old Victorian his and hers Tunnels Pools. I was totally on my own and it was great, despite cutting my foot on a sharp rock and dripping blood all the way back to the kiosk.

A few miles beyond Ilfracombe I arrived at Mortehoe. This place according to local legend is the last place that God made, and the first the devil will take, as it is so wild! The wind was buffeting the Bongo that night; or was it the devil hiding in the fog?

Broughton Burrows was my next stop. There was a young friendly car-park attendant there with a bright banana coloured VW, complete with surfboard on the roof. He had a comfortable job, chilling in a tiny wooden hut with his dog, phone, tablet and wood burner to keep warm. He told me that the shipwreck on the beach was a boat left by two Welshmen only three years ago. It looked much older, but that is the power of the sea.

I paid a short visit to Tapeley House, the mansion and gardens belonging to the anarchic billionaire Hector

Christie. The history room at the house has newspaper cuttings of all his protests against GM crops, Tony Blair and the Iraq War. The man himself was in the shop. I could tell it was him by the way the lady at the till went all gooey.

I walked to Clovelly from Buck's Mills as I was too tight to pay the entrance fee and wanted to approach the village naturally as opposed to be herded through the touristy Visitors Centre. The village is famous for its thatched roofs, narrow steep lanes and donkeys carrying luggage and supplies up and down the lanes. Amazingly, I managed to get some pictures with no one in the frames. This was because that day it was constant torrential rain, which incidentally looked great on the cobbles. On my way back, I met Phil Wells who was attempting to set a world record of walking 1000 miles barefoot. He was on crutches on a very stony path. We shook hands and I wished him well, then we went our separate ways.

I had to detour inland a little to meet up with friends Tina and Pigiron at the market town of Great Torrington. Whilst there, Tina and I went to a chilli festival and we tried the hottest chilli oil going. The seller reads you all the warnings about potential fits and panic attacks before sampling. At first, he refused to let us try it, because we were women, but we insisted and managed it fine, unlike the previous man who had cried for ten minutes after sampling. I had to buy some. Half a drop in hot chocolate keeps you warm for hours!

Back to the coast at Hartland Point, I camped at an eco site complete with a throne- designed earth closet. I must admit, I only stayed there because of the cool name "Loveland Farm".

Walking around South Hole, I came across another film crew for Channel 4 making a "Weird Weather" programme. I listened to four takes of the same sentence which did not tell me a lot and so I got bored and left.

I stayed two nights at Welcombe Mouth down a narrow remote lane. The only people about were four surfers and the surf was so strong, they even broke one of their boards. An early morning swim in the waterfall (just outside the van) set me up for the day beautifully.

Duckpool my next stop is an idyllic place and is, as the name suggests, a pool by the sea with a duck on. It was there that I met Mr Angry. He was stomping around saying "bloody typical" in a Cornish accent. I can only presume he was pissed off because I had parked in the place he wanted. By the time I returned from my walk he was leaving, accompanied by his very embarrassed wife.

I passed through the small seaside town of Bude, noting the pretty canal and old tramline that goes straight into the sea, and then Widemouth where I walked over the hill to Millook Haven where there is a lovely basic, isolated wooden house right by the beach. It is in an ideal spot as you cannot park there and so your peace would only be disturbed by walkers. I spent the evening watching a stunning sunset at Crackington Haven and camped up for the night at High Cliff on the moors. Just as dusk arrived so did a cracking thunderstorm. I spent a glorious night sat with my feet dangling out of the van watching the lightening embellish the moors and nearby valley.

The next day I was at Boscastle which was stuffed with day-trippers, but come 4.30pm, as if by magic, the village emptied. Whilst there I spoke to the local potter and went to the Witchcraft Museum which was great. It is full of artefacts and exhibits devoted to folk magic, ceremonial magic, freemasonry and Wicca.

Tintagel was my next meeting place with K. I had visited the castle there several times but a first for us were the intriguing ancient labyrinth rock carvings that we literally stumbled across by a derelict mill a few miles out of the village. During an evening drink outside the pub we met a couple, Phil and his girlfriend Guinevere. She was very spiritual and was in the area to discover where her name had originated. Guinevere was raised in a 40-year-old commune on the German/Swiss border and this was her very first holiday as an adult. This was because all the "tribe," as she described her family, work seven days a week all their life, so holidays were rarely taken. She was very interesting to talk to and I wanted to find out more, but she was worse for wear due to enjoying too much cider and kept having fits of giggles.

A visit to Trebarwith Strand with its natural caves and "washing machine" sea completed K's holiday. It is a lovely sheltered cove overlooking Gull Rock, way out at sea.

The Cornish surf was beckoning me, so when I saw a blow-up surfboard for sale, I bought it. Well, it is more like a kid's lilo with handles, but it worked to the standard I wanted anyway. I tried it out at a big surfer's beach but Loki got quite anxious looking for me in the big sea and nearly got run down by a RLNA Land rover, so I gave up and rescued her instead of practising my surfing skills. There were many opportunities for surfing in this area with terrific beaches such as Constantine and Booby Bay. It was there that I actually got a compliment off an RLNA bloke, who said I seemed to have the hang of surfing on my pretend surfboard!

The next day I did an eight-mile walk to the well-known Bedruthan Steps. Scattered along the sandy beach are several huge slate outcrops making a spectacular view from the cliff top. The massive surf crashing around them was very dramatic sight. Moving on, I called in to the surfing town of Newquay. It was too busy for my liking but not as commercial as I had imagined.

June 2014 – Trevaunance Cove to Plymouth

"If you don't know where you are going, any road will get you there"

Lewis Carroll

Around the tin mines at Wheal Coate, is a scary mine shaft that is so deep that it takes a stone six seconds to hit the water with a tremendous splash and then a thud as it hits the bottom. In the mist I came across two septuagenarians who were waiting for the mist to clear on top of the mountain. They had carried their huge hang gliders up there earlier. I was very impressed as I could only just lift up their gear.

The following morning I passed through Gwithian where I learned that the "Red Bull Storm Chasers" were in last year's storms, riding the biggest waves in the world (for five days). Apparently, they flew in with all their own lifeguards, boats and helicopters. Talk about the big boys arriving in town!

On an expensive campsite near St Ives, I encountered the most annoying Jobsworth site owner of the whole trip. Despite there being ample space overlooking the sea, he said I must park near the toilets. It was not a good start and it did not get any better. I had chosen this site as it provided a bus into St Ives, which suited me, as I wanted to visit the Tate museum without the dog. However, Mr Jobsworth tried to tell me that Loki was the responsibility of the site and I could not leave her in the well-ventilated van. I became quite angry stating that my dog is my responsibility and refused to budge off the bus. I visited the Tate and had a quick surf before returning to the site. My plan was to have a quick shower and then depart. He was in the ladies, and refused to let me have a shower as it was cleaning time. I kept calm, and informed him he had better leave as I was about to have a strip wash. He did, very reluctantly shouting "You've got 10 MINUTES". Perhaps we just had a character clash, but his attitude was downright rude! It was not acceptable to me, especially as it had cost £30 a night, and consequently I would not recommend this site to anyone.

On a walk down a steep path at Gurnards Head I met a lady called Caroline, who gave me a lift back up the hill in her purple Land Rover and then kindly invited me to stay at her place when I pass by Looe. More about that to follow.

I had to go to Lands End because it is the most westerly point of Cornwall but I did not like it as it is a huge hotel, tourist complex and theme park. Yuk!

However it was a significant stop on my journey and was quite memorable as I had walked a mile from Sennen Cove and got drenched. The place was swarming with soggy Japanese people nearly been blown off the cliffs. Even Loki was not impressed. I have a photo of her looking very wet and miserable under the famous signpost to prove it.

Having literally turned the corner, I was now moving up the coast. I stayed at Treen Farm for a few days as it was so lovely and one of my favourite sites. It has its own wood supply so you can have fires, also the local handy-man of the site lives in a proper tipi and organises foraging walks for the campers. The site is organised in such a way that it is easy to get to know people, very laid back and casual. Consequently I spent time with my neighbours, Ronnie, Meg, children, and Rosemary, who had a lilac VW van and a cat called Arthur. The amazing hidden cove of Pedn Vounder is a nearby nudist beach. I was met by a starkers Rosemary, a buxom lady, bouncing down the beach to meet me and help Loki down the very steep rocky cliffs. This amusing picture has been etched on my mind ever since! The sea was so rough, it was dangerous to swim in and I was dragged towards the swell, simply sitting in the surf. It was thanks to "strong" naked Rosemary that I was rescued out of the stunningly beautiful but dangerous sea.

The evening's entertainment was a short walk away over the cliffs to see the play "The importance of being earnest" at the Minack Outdoor Theatre. It just has to be experienced as the seascape backdrop is probably the best in Britain and the atmosphere wonderful.

Walking around the stunning cliffs the next day, I firstly had my picnic stolen by a seagull and then, I encountered a group of four hundred long distance fell runners... going in the opposite direction from me. They were running 44 miles over the mountains, well impressive, but very annoying when there are so many of them getting in your way on the tiny coastal path. I initially made an effort to get out of their way but Loki just stood there blocking the path just looking gormless.

On my walk to Tater Du lighthouse in the woods, I met a German couple who thought that I lived in the lighthouse. I was not sure how to take that, as a compliment or an insult that I looked like a lighthouse keeper. I guess I appeared both rugged and weather beaten or maybe just healthy to them.

My next stop for the night, simply because I liked the name was at the "Merry Maidens" the Neolithic stone circle a little inland. They are also known as "Dawns Men". Whatever, I woke up near them the next day.

I spent a few hours at Mousehole my favourite place being the "Rock Pool Café" overlooking the tidal pool which was unfortunately too rough to swim in. Travelling on through Penzance I went in search of camping gas at Newlyn. I found a supplier and moved on to Marazion campsite. It was a beautiful sunset, so I sat outside the pub enjoying a lovely Campari and soda. The next day I visited St Michael's Mount with all the other tourists. I wandered through the exotic gardens with Loki, pausing to relax and enjoy the hot sunshine. Returning from the Mount I waded through the sea over the causeway which was lovely and cooling.

Further east, Prussia Cove is a lovely area to camp. Here there are numerous small rocky coves in which to swim. The lord of the estate had built his own pizza oven but he was not overfriendly when I enquired about it. I only lost my van keys once on the journey and it was when I went swimming there, down by the rocks and near a group of young fishermen. I was so relieved to find them, as I thought they may have thrown them into the sea for a lark.

Around the Penzance area at Kynance Cove I explored an extraordinary deep lagoon hidden in the rocks. I managed to swim there just before the locals arrived. The beach is very picturesque with interesting rock formations scattered in the sand. Nearby, Henry's Campsite is homely, friendly and artistic. It is run by a mature hippie (not called Henry but Ron) who had built his own amphitheatre from rocks and a fire pit where he puts on live music. I met up with K again and on the Saturday night, we listened to Russian folk songs whilst avoiding the smouldering liquid of cooked marshmallows. Clueless children were tossing these lethal weapons about down by the fire.

We celebrated the summer solstice in a field at Mawgan where by chance we attended a charity concert. It was all going well until a very special teenager broke her ankle and complained that the vibrations of the music were making her pain worse. The consequence of this was that the whole fete and music stopped abruptly which I though was well over the top and unnecessary, especially as it meant less money for Great Ormond Street Hospital.

K left the following day so I was back to wild camping again. After asking permission from the farmer at Menabilly to stay the night, I walked to Polridmouth Cove where Daphne du Maurier used to go skinny-dipping; it was beautiful. On return to the van, a dog walker informed me that it was "illegal" to camp there. You can guess my smug reply and imagine how his ego started to deflate when I informed him that I had already spoken to the farmer.

On a friendlier note, the next day I ended up having a real coffee and chat in the van with a couple of students Ben and Paul who were doing their own 100 mile walk for themselves. Paul was doing a sustainable agricultural course and was having a huge rant about supermarkets. He definitely shared my hatred of the "devils shop". Next, I camped a few days with Caroline, the lady I had previously met at Gurnards Head. On arrival, she promptly gave me a map of her seventy-acre "estate" and disappeared. Four hours later, we shared a meal in her coach house, drinking homemade wine straight from the demi-john. She was a very interesting lady who sees herself simply as guardian of her land. She has many eco-like minded people sharing her land, who also live a back-to-basic life-style. On her hill, she had built a homemade stone labyrinth that was now becoming a bit overgrown but was still intriguing. The next day, I fought my way through the woods and undergrowth to her "beach". It was quite interesting experience, attempting to abseil down a steep cliff with a dog on a lead.

July 2014 – Bolberry Downs to Hordle

"Travel is not about leaving our homes, but leaving our habits"

Poci-Iyer

At Plymouth, I actually stayed in town at the Stoke Inn Brit Stop. It turned out that the landlord lived one street away from me in London a few years ago. As the pub was not doing food, I had a "slap down meal" from the local chippy and spent the rest of the evening talking with all the very friendly bar staff and locals. Julia had three jobs, Charlie worked on the docks and Jim, who kept buying me drinks, had an extremely small personal body space due to his learning disability.

The following morning, I went down to the Hoe for a coffee and looked around the huge lido and man made pools along the front. I really liked this place as I found it spacious and full of character.

Moving on, I drove to Thurlestone with a view over the cliffs to impressive Burgh Island and its posh art-deco hotel. As it was hot and I laid down in the long grass and had a snooze. Next thing I know, there was a commotion by me. Two girls had thought I had collapsed and were worried. I think it was because I appeared to have lain down in the recovery position, which incidentally is very comfortable!

The next evening I was at East Prawle in the Pigs Nose Pub. It is a proper junk emporium, stuffed floor to ceiling with antique and arty interesting stuff. It was a friendly place and I got talking to a group of locals about the pubs unusual décor.

I stayed the night in Torquay catching up with relatives, Ray and Sue, and christened their bath (which they had not used in five years as they do not like baths; very strange.) We had a meal at the Devon Dumpling, a pub with a very sexist sign depicting a woman with very large breasts. The sign had most likely been there for decades and accepted so it seemed pointless to remark upon it.

Sidmouth was full of foreign students partying and I got talking to a man who told me how he had "weekend custody" of his dog (how bizarre) and later I enjoyed further company in the colourful sunny town of Lyme Regis where I met up with friends who I used to work with, Luke, Lou and their baby Jake.

Past Seaton, I climbed the Gold Cap with terrific views everywhere. More in the wild, I camped at an out of the way car park and met a couple who were spending the night sleeping on the beach under the bright full moon. It was good to know that romance is still alive.

Chesil Beach had the only campsite in Britain with baths for single people, so I had to stay there. It is a lovely area and in the evening, I went for a long walk in search of phosphorescent plankton in the lagoon. Seeing it is a bit hit and miss; I got the miss bit! On Chesil beach I was relaxing and idly massaging the pebbles. This made me ponder about the laws of physics, and why there are no perfectly round marble-shaped pebbles on any of the beaches. There are numerous beautiful egg shapes, but never any spheres. I was becoming very philosophical.

Portland Point is quite wild and inhospitable. Despite this, there is present a shanty type village with many resident wooden huts. I was entertained by watching young lads tombstoning from the huge Pulpit Rock and having a whale of a time. Near Portland, I took a quick look at the "Verve", a citadel built in the 1840s by prisoners. Such an austere and horrible place; it is a huge dismal tunnel recently used to house illegal immigrants.

My ambition at Durdle Door was to swim through the arch and around it. In reality, the currents were too strong. I only managed to touch the arch and even Loki got spooked and made a hasty retreat to the nearby rocks. It is a stunning place, but during a walk further along the beach to Scratchy Bottom I had what could have been a fatal moment. I heard a thud behind me and it was a cluster of rocks fallen from the top of the cliff, only small ones, but enough to crack my skull if they had hit me. Therefore, I made another hasty retreat back (away from the cliffs).

Worth Matravers has a very interesting pub, the Cross & Compass, run by a man who is keen on both fossils and sculpture. The furniture in the garden consists solely of all his stone sculptures and inside he has developed his own fossil museum within the pub. It is also a no nonsense pub, drinks and pasties only and live music at the weekend.

Dancing Ledge nearby is a man made pool fashioned by the locals with dynamite in the 1920s. The ledge is the size of a ballroom. It is very tricky reaching it and I nearly fell down the cliff when Loki decided to panic half way back up. Luckily, I managed to keep my balance, got away with only a few bruises, and a sprained leg. Minor injuries for what could have been quite serious.

August 2014 – Lymington to Brighton (and the Isle of Wight)

"Tourists know where they have been. Travellers don't know where they are going"

Paul Theroux

I stayed a few days in Wareham at a family site with my K, daughter Lisa, her hubby Mark and kids, Lola and Dot. The nearby pub, the Silent Woman" was where we went for lunch. Amazingly, there were signs for no dogs OR CHILDREN in the pub itself, so we stayed in the garden where the kids found a dead rat!

After that, I spent a few days in the New Forest. No wild camping there and the sites were crowded, as you would expect in such a glorious place mid summer.

Isle of Wight

Unplanned, I decided to spend a week on the Isle of Wight as I had never been there before and I needed to slow down to keep to my string theory. Unfortunately, on my first day there, I slipped on a jetty and hurt my coccyx. So, when I got to Steephill Cove, a trendy beach, I splashed out and hired a deckchair for the whole day. Bliss for my bum. There, I met an elderly resident deck chair man, Dave Wheeler, who was 89 years old and sprightly with it. He was a real old character who kept the place tidy and would not let anyone get away with not paying for a deckchair. He had been an Island longshoreman for most of his life and lived in the village with other members of his family (and still does as far as I know).

Whilst camping at Whale Chine, the weather turned stormy and nearly flattened a few tents. Due to the ferocious wind the people next door had taken down their awning. It was a very cosy affair. There were two adults, Stuart, Lorraine and three big teenage kids all sleeping in an old VW van. They managed fine and made the most of their holiday despite the weather. Their neighbour who liked to be called "Seaside Steve" had entertained them the previous night with his kazoo and when I met the family, they gave the impression that they were hiding from him, in an attempt to avoid a repeat performance. I am sure he would be worth a listen. I covered most of the island visiting the affluent towns of Shanklin and Ventor but I preferred the wild southwest area. Walks from Culver and Tennyson Downs both had fantastic views of the island.

Back on the mainland, I spent half a day in Portsmouth walking most of the six-mile promenade, admiring The Spinnaker Tower and wandering around the old town.

After a day on Hayling Island, I arrived at Bognor Regis, where a man took a shine to Loki and bought her a bag of chips for some reason. He queued up for fifteen minutes for them, before rushing back to his workplace. K was joining me again and we stayed in a "Mickey Mouse" Hotel; not one of the best as it had no hot water, bath plug or even wine!

I was surprised to find out that this part of the coast is full of private estates such as Kingston. The coastal houses appear quite showy and decadent, set back from non-descript beaches by corridors of grass. Living in these gated communities seems so restricting; it would be like prison to me. There are signs everywhere, no picnics, games, bikes, caravans, boats, trailers or washing on display. Therefore, it was quite refreshing when I arrived at Goring on Sea where people are encouraged to enjoy themselves by having BBQs and picnics on the grass.

After this, I went forward to Brighton to have an enjoyable evening with a friend, Anje. I had my best veggie meal so far on my travels at the well-established and wonderful vegetarian restaurant, Terre à Terre.

Returning west along the coast I got back on track. It was Bank Holiday so extremely busy at West Wittering. Despite this, I spent a great day at East Head, a large nature reserve on the estuary watching numerous flocks of birds, and took to lolling in the sand dunes and laughing at kids having mud fights.

September 2014 – Littlehampton to Tollesbury

> "I don't know where I am going, but I am on my way"
>
> **Carl Sagan**

I began this month with bed and baths at a friend's flat in Littlehampton. Parents, Luke and Lou were getting baby Jake acclimatised to the sea. For me, it was lots of swimming, walking, eating, drinking and relaxing. Most memorable was a belly dancer who got all but one of us up to jiggle along with her, on the night out at the local Turkish restaurant.

After a week of luxury, I was back in the Bongo continuing my eastern route through Cuckmere Haven where there are great sunset views over the Sussex coast. I returned to Seaford front for the night. There I got chatting to a neighbour in a van. The man, Aldo, said that he admired my balls for travelling alone and then got all embarrassed at what he had said, which was amusing! He also told me about something on the web that had gone viral; It was about heating a van up with a nightlight and two plant pots. Personally, I was not convinced so I never properly looked into it.

The walk from Birling Gap up the Seven Sisters and back, hence 14 Sisters, is stunning, but very knackering; even Loki was nearly buckling towards the end. Beachy Head is invigorating on a windy day and I am pleased that they now have resident counsellors there to support anyone thinking of jumping off the cliff.

Near Norman's Bay, there is a very old (1405) pub called the Star Inn, an old sluice house originally. I took Loki for a £6 carvery. She had the lot: red, white and brown meat and she was understandably ecstatic.

At Cooden Beech, I parked up and came across a private beach party. My contribution was some wine and logs that I had been carrying around since South Wales. Nick, Jasper, Tab and Jode, to name a few, were seeing to the music and fire, whilst the women just chilled. It was one good night, and an annual celebration for them, as they get permission from the man who owns the beach.

At Bexhill, I visited hairdressers for a trim. The hairdresser thought I would have to have all my hair shaved off when she first inspected it, as it felt so damaged and wiry to her. When I told her it was full of sand as I had just emerged from the sea, she realised why it felt like a brillo pad. Anyway, I had it cut and felt better, even if it did not look it. I met up briefly with my niece, Ellie, next to the lovely De La Warr art nouveau pavilion and then caught a local train to see a live band on the front at Hastings.

Camber Sands had gone upmarket since I was last there years ago. I was glad to be on a proper sandy beach and I made the most of it by going swimming three times.

I paused at Dungeness, a nuclear facility, surrounded by a wooden village and I was spooked by the humming sound. It was very, very strange. A discussion with people confirmed that it had only been heard this last week and they were as confused about it as I was. I found out later, that it was probably the ships taking supplies out to the wind farm out at sea. Therefore there was nothing too weird or nuclear about it as I had thought.

Folkestone was another place where I came across a private rave in the woods by the beach. The weather the following day was quite ethereal, like a primordial magic mist. Swamps, groans and stagnant pools: I almost expected a dinosaur to wander up to me.

As K was with me in Broadstairs, we stayed in a hotel and the beautiful room where Charles Dickens wrote "Nicholas Nickleby" (apparently). Then on my own again through Margate where I visited the unusual

Victorian shell grotto. The shelled walls and ceilings are all black due to the candle fumes. Further on, I arrived at Whitstable renowned for its trendy shops and expensive oyster bars. It was impossible to park up so I did not stay.

In the marches, near Seasalter, I was camped by the sea only to be awakened at 5am by what I named the "Lugworm Club". Four blokes armed with forks and buckets, they were shouting to each from their cars for at least 40 minutes before setting off for worms. It is obviously a social thing.

On Grain Island there is a place called Horrible Hill with several theories about why the area has that name. Rumour has it that in Napoleonic times, prisoner boats were moored there

and you could hear the prisoners' wails. Possibly, also in the 15th century, the place was used as a gallows and you could hear the screams of the people to be hung. At one time it was used as a pig farm and the smell of manure was horrible apparently. In later days there was a chemical factory there that also stunk. All pretty horrible I would agree.

After Horrible Hill, it all went horribly wrong for me too!

I did not plan to drive through Central London! I had intended to cross the Thames at the Dartford Crossing, but somehow missed it. Consequently I ended up driving through the Blackwell Tunnel, past the O2 during the rush hour. I was only about four miles from home in Sydenham and despite my panic in fast traffic, I carried on - no way could I give up. I got off the fast road at my first opportunity at Aveley and drove down by the Thames for what seemed like ages towards Corringham. I found a sweet spot to park up near a small oil terminal and the following morning I drove to Fobbing, a posh village, and had my breakfast in the van overlooking Canvey Island.

After that experience I was even more determined to stick to the small roads and out of the way places. Two Tree Island is a huge nature reserve only reached across a bridge. I had neighbours, Hadyn and Margaret from

Wales, who provided me with company in a funny way. Hadyn was boasting about his travelling experiences and said they would "protect me from the goings on late into the night". This meant any cars that visited the island after dark. Out to sea, the necklace of red and green lights across the Thames looked quite pretty.

Passing the Southend-on-Sea plastic palms and arcaded frontage, the marshes were looming. It was duck heaven around this area and Burton on Crouch was recovering from the previous night's carnival; it was all over but I did manage to catch the tail end fireworks.

October 2014 – Tolleshunt Major to Sutton Beach

"Life is either a daring adventure or nothing"
Helen Keller

Tollesbury has an old tidal swimming pool called Woody's Pool built in 1907, which I used twice, and wedged in the marshes is an impressive bright red lightship which retired in 1988. It is now used for activity holidays. There is a maze of paths around it and you must be very careful walking around the quagmire of muddy paths which can be totally submerged at high tide.

I did not stay at West Mersea but stopped to admire rows of colourful beach huts and the beach which is full of shimmering oyster shells.

Clacton was very busy with five TV crews on the front parade interviewing the candidate for the coming bi-election. As I walked along the promenade, I realised I may have made it onto national TV, along with the loony candidate wandering around in his canary yellow suit and a beer in hand.

The start of October means that Loki can go on any beach in the country. Nevertheless, for me, it is another story; it means easier parking, but closed museums, and more importantly closed toilets, which is a bit inconvenient (pun!).

I stayed at Frinton on Sea, which is well posh with lots of bistros, and beach huts on stilts, there is even a thatched public toilet by the beach. The neighbouring Walton on Naze is totally opposite, with a few charity shops and basic cafes, but I did manage to buy my camping gas there.

Past Harwich, I travelled round the River Stour and stopped at Shotley Gate for the night, just outside a friendly local, The Bristol Arms. The blokes at the bar were amicable and helpful informing me of places further up the Norfolk coast. The following morning, a mobile greasy spoon had parked next to me. The owner humbly apologised in case he had disturbed me early on which I thought was very thoughtful. In the same area is the small HMS Ganges Museum. It was a training ship for the navy involving kids as young as 11 years old. I learned all about ditty bags (a bag for odds and ends used by sailors and fishermen) and button boys. These were young daredevils who climbed the masts at displays carried out by naval training establishments and balanced on the tiny button platforms or even from the masts themselves. The museum has an impressive photograph of about 70 young sailors performing this spectacle.

Northwards, on the River Orwell, Pinmill is a quiet trendy hamlet with a pub the Butt & Oyster and several residential Old London barges. It was a different experience parking up for the night at Felixstowe adjacent to the docks. All night long, giant cranes were hauling the enormous shipping containers onto the massive ships. These were leaving to traverse all parts of the globe. Many people come here to view the ports activities, staying the night in their vans. I met up with a couple, Liz and Jay from Norfolk and Sparky who used to be a pilot, escorting the ships into and out of the port.

Driving on after two nights at the port I headed back into the middle of nowhere, Shingle Street. This place consists of a few isolated cottages on a wild beach full of sea cabbages. It was quite atmospheric in the howling wind, vertical drizzle and wild seas. Only the odd crazy windsurfer was visible in the mist. I left this lonely place to camp the night at Shottisham campsite. I had a glass of wine at the nearby Sorrel Horse pub, which had been bought by the villagers and run as a co-operative. Warming my toes by the log fire, I listened to "bloke talk" for an hour before returning to the van to sleep.

The bad weather continued, so I was Bongo bound at Orford Quay for a good while watching the fishermen gut their catch under a makeshift tarpaulin. However, a day later, and the sun shone through the giant golden shell sculpture on the beach near Thorpeness. The converted water tower "House in the Clouds" is visible for miles around and attracts many tourists as it is so unusual. The weather remained changeable over the next few days with lots of wind, rain and rainbows over the extensive nature reserve. At Walberswick hundreds of geese were arriving from Canada, an incredible sight. There are crow scarers in the fields but the geese just get used to the gunfire and end up playing on the machines.

I think the most unusual pier so far was Southwold. This is because of the "under the pier" amusements which are all Victorian and hilarious. There was constant laughter due to the silly games like crossing the motorway as a granny with a Zimmer, or trying to avoid being swotted as a fly. It is difficult to describe, but well worth a visit for its uniqueness.

Purely by chance, I parked up outside the bowling club at Lowestoft. A plaque informed me that it was the most easterly bowling club in the UK. A significant point for my travels I thought.

I never realised that Great Yarmouth is a spit of land wedged between the broads and the river. I spent the day doing "fishing" museums to shelter from the rain. I went out of town for the night to Caister on Sea where the coastguard man told me stories of stupid parents who dig holes in the dunes and then put their small children in them!

For the night, I paid £5 to park up at the Brit Stop - Old Hall Hotel, Caister. The price included entry into their spa, so I made use of the facilities and enjoyed a swim, jacuzzi, steam room and cold plunge pool. The only downside is that I was awoken at 6am by the early Aldi deliveries.

Just a few miles down the road on the edge of a cliff is the tiny hamlet of California. I had a field to myself camping and the roar of the waves was deafening. A tiny curlew escorted me down the blustery beach and later Simon befriended me .He was a young man from Leeds who was very talkative and it was quite difficult to break away from him.

It was near California that I gave a facelift to the Bongo. With my poor reversing skills, I had badly dented the rear bumper and it began to annoy me. Having had a £250 quote from a garage, I had decided that I had to live with it. However I found a tiny garage near California to do the repair for £25 and they even gave me sandpaper to finish it off before repainting. Maybe I have not lost all of my charm after all!

Early morning at Horsey I woke up to the sound of shouting geese. This would be a familiar sound for the next few weeks in the marshes. I spotted several seals on the nearby beaches. These were becoming more and more deserted the further north I travelled and as time went on.

At Sea Palling, the lifeboats list of achievements was quite surprising. They had rescued many people over the years but also a dog and even a dead horse.

All the villages in this area are literally hugging the coast and falling into the sea, especially Happisburgh where a road literally ends over the cliff. It was where 500 people lost their lives in the 1953 floods.

Cromer was the biggest town I passed after Yarmouth. I spent the night here at the top of the town - well out of the way. I wandered the narrow streets past the pier, pavilion and posh Hotel de Paris with its smart copper turrets. My destination was the White Lion Pub where I caught live music. It was not great, what I call wedding music, but the band did have a mature female punky sax player who was my favourite band member. Around this area of Norfolk the parking fees were astronomical, together with their intimidating notices. I found out from the toilet cleaner that they hire private security firms who check the car parks hourly. Buggered if I would pay £2.50 for the privilege of having my breakfast in one (because of the view!), so I moved on. Incidentally, I had parked on the front all night where there were no restrictions or interferences.

Sherringham area is a bit hilly, so I enjoyed the vertical walk up the cliff path. The Funky Mackerel Café sells unusual flapjacks - Bombay Mix flavour that tastes a bit like curried custard - not unpleasant.

Later that day I took a lovely long walk down Holkam beach. It is an enormous expanse of sand with hundreds of varying colourful beach huts, some on stilts with a beautiful pine forest as a backdrop.

I stayed the night at Deepdale backpacker's site where, for triple the price I paid, you could stay in a wigwam. Brancaster Staithe used to have the largest malt house in Britain in the 1800s. Now it has a pub The Jolly Sailor that specialises in unusual rums and pizzas.

The weather by now was quite unpredictable, very cold and windy most of the time. Occasional sunshine allowed me to get some good photos of the colourful red and white cliffs of Hunstanton. Being almost constantly cold and wet made me invest in a tiny fan heater for when I find a campsite open. I am learning not to stay in the cold too long as I cannot get properly warm again. I warmed up with a couple of rums at the Seafront Bar, decorated with over the top Halloween decorations. I counted 15 ghosts, 3 cadavers, a giant spider and movement sensitive ghouls that moved and talked when you passed them. You can buy them just down the road in the town at the "biggest joke shop in Britain" for an astronomical price.

By now most of the toilets were closed, and so it was getting more difficult to fill up my water container. I have even had to resort to graveyards occasionally!

I breakfasted a few days later on the Queen's Estate at Sandringham. The gardens are very beautiful as you would expect and the house looks quite interesting. In the stables, you feel like you are wandering around her garage full of all her old but desirable cars.

I entered Lincolnshire over the very old swing bridge at Sutton Bridge. It has now become tricky parking by the roadside due to the deep ditches on both sides. In the marshes near Gedney Drove End there are big signs warning you about unexploded bombs and missiles. According to a local, the RAF can shoot at you if you are in their way whilst they are practising. I was not very keen on this area as it is quite uninspiring with only dykes, mud and millions of cabbages. Walking the long dykes in the wind is a bit like exercising on a treadmill. I found it quite depressing, but maybe it was the bad weather that made me feel so negatively about the area. On the foraging front and growing wild, I found out about sea beet, similar to spinach and very hot mustard plants, both edible.

My sister, Kath and husband Ian met up with me at the town of Boston and so I stayed in a hotel with them. The town is known to be a little edgy due to the influx of Eastern Europeans there working in the fields and some people not wanting them there, but I did not come across any racism, just a geezer called Andy. He gave us his life story about a Thai wife and exotic places he had lived. His pub looked as if all sorts of dark deals went on behind closed doors, geezer deals! The following morning I shared the panoramic views with my sister from the top off the impressive Stump church tower before departure.

Skegness is not really my cup of tea, endless caravans, pleasure beaches and hotels. However further north, you reach deserted beaches again. Anderby Creek has a few interesting sculptures scattered around, including a "cloud bar", where you can watch the clouds go by whilst lounging on special stone sculptured seats.

Sutton on Sea, felt a little dismal. The beach sheds are made of bricks and breeze blocks, all grey and in need of a lick of paint. There, I bought myself some wellies and to save space, I trimmed them down. They are very comfortable too, and I do not care if I look like an overgrown child in them (as they have stars on).

November 2014 –Kilnsea to North Berwick

"Once a year, go someplace you have never been before"

Dalai Lama

Mablethorpe was my next stop. It is a typical seaside town with a vast sandy beach. I joined the tourists on the cute sand train that takes you miles across the estuary. The next stop was Donna Nook, the nature reserve where I again joined the crowds to go and see the seals and their white pups lolling about on the beach. There were about fifteen pairs present, lolling about the beach seemingly oblivious to the curious humans.

Through Grimsby and across the Humber Bridge and Hull I headed for Spurn Head and Withernsea. The only remaining part of the pier here is a castle like entrance by the promenade. They gave up on repairs after the pier kept getting rammed by boats. The last straw was when a ship cut it clean in two and half the pier floated away to sea!

The clocks went back, so now it was getting dark really early on, which made the evenings longer. I got quite down as a result, but a visit from K cheered me up. A scupper to my travel plans also unnerved me. I lost my tenants in my house in Wales, hence their rent money to subsidise my travel budget was in jeopardy. K was also anxious about the logistics of how he would be able to meet up with me when faraway in northern Scotland. We worked it out together and moved on.

The wind was now getting bitterly cold, so a treat of a hotel at Flamborough Head was well appreciated. The regular staff at the North Star Hotel were very friendly and the place itself seemed quite old fashioned but homely.

Back in the Bongo, the weather turned atrocious and even the inside of the Bongo was muddy. I managed to dry off eventually at the campsite at Filey Brigg, using my fan heater. This allowed me to later enjoy a walk along the Brigg, which has an almost lunar type landscape. It is a wild place, where the sea is always calm on one side and rough on the other. It was quite moody in the mist.

I drove through Scarborough into Hayburn Wyke where, unfortunately, I came a cropper. Whilst climbing a fence, I fell and twisted my knee. The image of me was with my knee in the air stuck in the fence and my body on the ground. Ouch! Even Loki yelped as I had kicked her on the way down. So, I had to have a quiet moment for the pain to recede. A group of school kids passed by and cheered me up. I asked a girl of about eight years old if she was enjoying her day, to which she boldly replied in a broad Yorkshire accent, "Ay, but that's nowt. Got a whole week off without parents," she said smugly. She made me chuckle.

I was unable to walk due to my minor injury, so I parked up at Ravenscar by a hotel overlooking Robin Hood's Bay with it scarred beach landscape. I managed to hobble to the hotel for a coffee and it felt weird seeing Christmas decorations and tree, as I had managed to avoid anything pertaining to Christmas up to then. I decided to rest my leg and stay the following night at Whitby Youth Hostel. The hostel is situated next to the stunning Abbey ruins overlooking the town and river Esk. It was a lovely sunset, so I got some great shots of the monstrously beautiful abbey; I can see why it was an inspiration for Dracula. Whitby Town was displaying the remnants of its annual Goth weekend a few days before and a local lady thought the Bongo looked like a Gothmobile.

Moving up to Brunswick Bay, a small pretty village with lots of holes in the cliffs, Loki nearly came to an abrupt end chasing a pheasant over a cliff. Fortunately, she responded to my screams of "NO". She also nearly fell down a huge quay wall and was hanging on with her front paws - like a canine cartoon character. Luckily, she was able to pull herself up. It made me realise that her sight at dusk was not as good as I thought, so I needed to be more careful with her from now on.

I spent a night at Skinningrove, which is quite a raw but characterful place and the friendly Moonfleet pub. Despite the coldness of the water, I went swimming by the deserted Quay at Cattersty Sands. It was here that two women, Barbara and Kate, thought I was trying to commit suicide when they saw me enter the sea and Loki did not follow me. I warmed up after with a hot water bottle and some hot chocolate and chilli drink.

Saltburn is a lovely Victorian town built on the cliff top with a naked pier; one that has no amusements cafes or fortune tellers on it. The original smugglers village is down below where, on the long beach one hundred years ago, Donald Campbell set the world speed record of 350mph.

Unsure if I was having a bit of cabin fever, I found myself talking to my knees (praising their good health) and being spooked by my red tin cup. It started "singing", sounding as if a baby bird was trapped in it. I must get out more I thought!

I drove on to South Shields mining area through thick fog, so I was unable to see the famous transporter bridge at Hartlepool. Stopping at Ryehope, I asked a man the way to the beach to which he replied, "that way, but its crap". I thought I would make my own mind up and yes, he was perfectly right. It was the worst beach of my travels due to it consisting of 100% compounded coal dust. This is courtesy of our forebears who dumped the coal into the sea in 1937. At Roker, I had a look around the engine museum. It was closed for winter, but the bloke maintaining it showed me around and even made me a cup of tea. That is typical good old northern hospitality!

My next Brit Stop was the Robin Hood pub in Yarrow. This place was on GMTV during the World Cup as it had been completely plastered in English flags. They even televised the blokes tearing them down when the English team lost. There I met Katherine, the helpful barmaid, a lady drowning her sorrows after an argument with her partner, and a cosmologist.

The following day was not a very good one as the alternator belt on the van broke. It was very noisy and scary as I was unsure what was wrong, imagining the worst scenario. Could this mean a dead Bongo, and possibly the end of the journey? Predictably, the AA man rescued me and took me to a garage to fix it. The only down side was that I had to travel about 30 miles back on fast roads in the dark, both of which I hated. I managed to get back on track and bedded down for the night by the side of a quiet road about to have my tea when I saw this brilliant bright light shining on the van from outside.

I knew immediately that it was the police. On opening the door, amazingly Loki started growling. "Patricia Heaven, are you doing a bit of wild camping?" I felt quite "tagged" my obscure freedom exposed, but they must have had a bit of a chuckle when they discovered my age (60) as I guess they were expecting youngsters. Anyway, they were friendly enough and suggested they find me somewhere better to stay. Without further ado, they found me a "safer" place for the night in a café yard. Consequently, I got a very fast police escort into Cresswell village. The kind thought was there, but I had a very restless night, as the nearby huge security light made it feel as if I was sleeping in a golfing range. It had been an eventful few days and this was the only time that I was "moved on" by anybody during the whole of my trip.

It was at Lower Newton, a tiny hamlet with just a pub in the middle of nowhere, that I nearly got my first parking fine, as the ticket had fallen below my Christmas decorations on the dashboard. I successfully appealed but there was no apology. Keen to get more miles under my belt I passed through Craster and Beadnell, stopping the night at Seahouses. I warmed up in the typical Olde Ship Inn. It has a nautical theme as you may expect and is full of artefacts such as model fishing boats, diving helmets, branding irons and lamps. Sat in the galley sipping my warming mulled wine I felt I could have been on a real ship. The weather was fine, but by now but it was getting cold even in the van. My best friend was now definitely my hot water bottle with a routine of hands, back, bum, tum and feet. Back was definitely the most comforting.

I had been looking forward to reaching Holy Island for ages. I have visited here before, but wanted to explore it properly. It is such a magical place that I spent two days there, walking around and taking photos as the weather was by now reasonable. The head nun of the Priory, Teresa, kindly gave me some water (not holy) and I met a man, Jim, who was doing proper wild camping by the causeway with his tiny tent and bicycle. It made my own journey seem quite luxurious.

The causeway is quite spectacular and the tide also very swift. The sign by the road says "Be Responsible," and you must be, otherwise you could float away out to sea. I was only gone five minutes taking photos and when I looked back the Bongo was 6 inches under water. Yes,

I did panic a bit, especially as Loki was dawdling along in her usual way.

Back on the mainland at Redskin Cove, there was a couple carrying armfuls of seaweed back to their car. I was curious, so I asked why. It was their intention to bathe in it for joint pain. They did not appreciate it when I said they would smell like a fish and were more concerned with slipping on it. Still, it made a funny mental picture in my head. Whilst there, I also saw some eider ducks, and found a £20 note on the beach!

Berwick upon Tweed is a memorable town with its huge ramparts overlooking the town. It is the last town of England despite on-going battles with the Scots in the 15 Century. It was also a favourite place for the artist Lowry, and a trail identifies certain buildings from his paintings.

Arrival in Scotland

At last on 26th November 2014 I reached Scotland. Crossing the border seemed all a bit unimpressive, just a quite scruffy Scottish flag and a "Welcome to Scotland" notice by the side of the road. It felt quite pertinent to me, as I would be spending the rest of this year and a big part of 2015 in Scotland. Keen to get off the A1, I took the first lane turning right and ended up in a tiny fishing hamlet down an extremely steep narrow windy lane: Lower Burnmouth. It is nestled below the steep cliffs only visible from a boat and is really two rows of cottages and nothing else. It was very peaceful so I found the harbourmaster, measuring his fishing nets, and asked permission to stay the night. He said it was fine for £20, jokingly. That must be, the £20 that I found on the beach a few days ago! He warned me that the fishing boats could be noisy and they leave at 5am so I may be disturbed. In reality, it was 3am when I woke. However, I had a lovely peaceful evening watching the fishermen hosing down their boats and a pair of resident swans gliding coolly around the harbour.

On my visit to Eyemouth, whilst stocking up with food supplies, I entered a scruffy pet shop. Somehow I got locked in with the shopkeeper, who was very embarrassed. It took him 30 minutes to release me as he had to remove the whole mortice lock. I tried to make jokes about how I did not think I would be spending Christmas in a pet shop but he was not amused. Perhaps he was scared of me, something that I will never know.

Out of the town the walk to St Abbs Head was wonderful with its unusual rock features and at Petticoat Bay, I saw about 20 baby seals with two adult minders. They were making spooky ghostly noises that I had read are quite normal for youngsters calling their mothers. St Abbs village has one of the 12 striking sculptures depicting the losses of fishermen in the severe 1889 storm, when there were 189 deaths up and down the Scottish coast. The sculptures are small but very moving - the wives and children are all looking longingly out to sea, in search of their lost family.

Nearby, I went on a four mile drive well out of the way and a long walk to Fast Castle ruins; a 15th century coastal fortress. The cliff was shrouded in mist and I only just made it back to the van before dark, a bit dodgy on the cliffs but a great place to spend the night. The following evening I was back in civilisation at Pease Bay, overlooking the bay and at the campsite, I treated myself to a cheap meal. The site was deserted as you may expect for that time of the year. Nearby, Cove Bay is a small village with a tiny old derelict fishing harbour below. You can only access it by passing through a tunnel cave so it is quite picturesque.

Ness Point is not so pretty due to the nearby cement factory. It was a dead end road and so I had to turn around in a traveller's camp. The camp was unfortunately unkempt and disgusting, with dirty nappies outside the caravans and rubbish strewn across the road. Dunbar is an old looking town boasting several grand old stone buildings. I visited the museum that informed me that John Muir the explorer and nationalist was born there. Close by I visited Tantallon Castle ruins and Seacliff beach where there is a secret hidden quay with fine views across to Bass Rock.

December 2014 – Aberlady Bay to Stonehaven

> "We travel not to escape life, but for life not to escape us"
>
> **Anonymous**

It was the beginning of December and I decided it was time to go for another swim. It was sunrise and beautiful at North Berwick. I met a young man, Blair, in the Ship Inn who was a bit worse for wear and would not stop talking. I learned all about his family and his ulcerated leg which he insisted on showing me on his phone - why do people do this?

The Law is the huge conical hill that is visible for miles around. It is there to be climbed, so I did. The view was a little misty but still a fantastic climb and it warmed me up. My next night was spent at Aberlady Bay which is a bird sanctuary with endless dunes. It was my ideal spot, the only down side was that I had to walk alone as dogs are not allowed. Close to Edinburgh I needed facilities, so I stayed at a campsite at Prestopans. The nearby museum highlights include the remains of a Hoffman kiln and a Cornish Beam Engine, relics of the early coal mining carried out by the Newbattle monks in the 13th Century, arguably the first instance of British coal mining.

K was joining me again at Edinburgh for a short "city break". We stayed in a strange B&B that was all pink inside, with Italian waiters who served breakfast in kilts. I love the city's higgledy-piggledy buildings and meandering lanes full of character and life. We did all the usual walks up Arthur's Seat and surrounding hills and finished off with a visit to the Royal Yacht Britannia.

The nights had definitely drawn in by now, with sunset at approx 4pm. I departed Edinburgh later than expected so it was pitch black when I set off across the busy Forth Bridge, and consequently I had no choice other than to park up in a golf club car park for the night. Strange buzzing sounds in the night turned out to be a small nearby oil terminal near Inverkeithing.

Passing through quite industrial towns just past Kirkcaldy I parked up in the harbour at Dysart Village. Then it started snowing. For once, I was not hoping for a white Christmas, but time to stock up on thermals, I thought. Despite my wishes, the next morning I woke up to a white landscape. I drove gingerly to East Wemyss to look at the prehistoric caves with paintings inside and Mc Duff castle ruins, both of which were quite unusual.

The next part of the coast was almost wall-to-wall golf links but my next destination was the small village of Elie. The roads were white with horizontal sleet, but I arrived safely and went to investigate the nearby Lady's Tower. This was where, in Victorian times, Lady Anstruther would bathe nude in Riley Bay and ring the tower bell to inform people to stay away... or not? It really was cold now and the windscreen was full of ice, but I still managed to walk to the beginning of the Ellie Chain walk, however traversing the chain walk is impossible with a dog. It is literally hanging onto chains around the cliff and in and out of caves. Not for the faint hearted, but I will definitely return at some time to do the chain walk. I needed to warm up at yet another Ship Inn by the harbour, a very old inn with a roaring log burning stove. My short sojourn there was unfortunately spoiled by what I can only label as "Golfing Wankers", ignorant, loud self obsessed men in Rupert Bear trousers who ignore your requests for them to move out of the way to enable you get to the fire and bar and back. I did manage to push my way past them but was fuming. The following morning it was so cold that the windscreen inside and out was thick with ice and I relied on my thermals and hot water bottle to keep warm.

Anyway, my next stop was at Pittenweem. What a lovely name! Here is a hermits cave, the hermit "apparently" had a luminous arm so he could read and write in the cave - well handy.

I managed to find a farm campsite open at Crail the next night where there were no showers but I was toasty warm in the van with my little fan heater. The elderly gentleman owner was watching his huge TV screen in his kitchen with the blinds open. I was a bit bored and curious about the programme. I did think about watching his TV through my binoculars, but decided that that would be unethical!

The weather was now cold, -2 degrees, but at least dry, so I was able to walk around the coastal path over the next few days. I stayed at Kingbarnes, a lovely sandy bay. Nearby Cambo mansion and grounds pander to the rich golfing folk. I went a lovely walk near the grounds and came across some wild pigs snoozing in the bushes surrounded by an electric fence. Loki was unaware of this and I suddenly heard her yelping like mad. She was fine but literally a bit shocked. Two locals, Ann and Andy, met me on the beach and informed me of the local history. They invited me for a cup of tea and warned me that the car park had been used for dogging in the Summer time. I told them that I was not worried as it was far too cold now for all that business!

Amazingly the sun came out the following morning so I watched the sunrise over the sea from my bed. So cool! A few miles inland I went to find a Celtic cross carved into the rock face at Dunino Den. Some ancient stone steps lead down to a stream. It is an ancient pagan site that, according to folklore, was used for human sacrifice by the druid priests. As usual the trees were full of ribbons, but I still found it quite a magical place.

Back on the coast, another druid-meeting place is a huge red rock that you can climb. Budda Rock was where long ago, pirates would light fires to guide their boats back to land.

The first big town for ages was St Andrews, a charming place full of characterful buildings, and lively due to the university. After looking around the castle I made my way down to the Tentsmuir Forest and arrived just before dark. This was probably one of my favourite wild camping places as it was so huge and full of giant pine trees, frozen sand dunes and endless sandy beach. The silence was awesome, that was until I suddenly heard a tremendous roar sounding like a huge machine in the forest. Well, it was a plane taking off only a few miles away. I had forgotten that nearby is RAF Leuchars. After another take-off, the silence resumed. I was all alone, but at about 6.30pm (and well dark by then) a car drove up and parked next to me. By this time, I heard learned to be assertive, so I went up to the man in his car. He innocently informed me that the café was closing in two minutes. I never found the café... mysterious! The next morning, a walk over the frozen dunes led me to the sea which was calm as a millpond. It felt very bizarre, having no gales to contend with and such a stunning location.

In need of a laundry, I stayed at a campsite at Monifieth. It was here I got lots of attention and free drinks from the long-term residential caravan men. It seems that they had not seen a woman for about twenty years. Their accent was thick Scottish and they were quite tipsy. It was like being stuck in a room with half a dozen Rab C Nesbitts! All quite harmless, and luckily there was a man from Manchester who could translate for me.

Scattered fishing villages dot the coastline around, most famous being Arbroath for its smokies; which are delicious. I stayed at a beautiful sandy Lunan Bay and walked to Red Castle, which is associated with Richard the Lionheart. The tiny hamlet of Catterline has weird sculptured volcanic stacks on the beach. Hiding there was a baby white seal patiently awaiting its mother. It looked so vulnerable especially as the sea was wild and full of scary whirlpools.

Dunnottar Castle was closed for winter but I managed a cold windy walk up to the cliff to admire its beauty and stunning location on top of a gigantic rocky outcrop.

It was now coming up to Christmas. I had to go inland back up to Perth, to meet K at a campsite near Scone for the festive season. We had a very different Christmas day with a BBQ huddled under the frozen awning and then walked around the castle where the only life was a few wandering peacocks. We went inland to spend Boxing Day with friends Vic and Aide at their home in Carputh near Dunkeld. It was party time, surrounded by beautiful scenery. Moving back to the coast we stayed at a cottage for a few days at St Cyrus with its extensive sandy beach. I particularly enjoyed the cottage's "boudoir", i.e. a bathroom that is big enough to put all your stuff on the floor and with two luxurious baths.

We celebrated New Years Eve watching the Stonehaven Fireball Ceremony, which was brilliant. Wire cages are made up, and filled with combustible material, such as coal, nets, cork, rope and tar to waterproof it. Each cage has a three-foot wire handle to keep the flames away from the "swinger" but the spectators can be showered with the fall out sparks. The ceremony consists of a group of about 40 local men and women swinging the flaming wire cages around their head up and down the high street and ending with the cages being slung into the harbour to extinguish them. By this time, people are knackered so they do not reach far but it is a memorable way to celebrate Hogmanay. Stonehaven is also famous for its fish and chip shop, which was where the first ever Mars Bar was deep-fried, but I did not fancy one so gave that a miss and saw the New Year in with an Indian takeaway and bottle of bubbly back at the cottage with K.

January 2015 – St Cyrus to Dunnet

"Take only memories, leave no footprints"
Chief Seattle

It is traditional for me to have a New Year's Day swim in the sea so I returned to Catterline. K joined me reluctantly in the sea before returning home. The water was very cold so the dip was quick, but it was so refreshing and exhilarating. I had been a bit reluctant to leave the warmth of the cottage at St Cyrus, but also happy to be on the road again.

I drove through Aberdeen to Balmedie Country Park. It was a beautiful sunset and a full moon was rising. Eighteen ships were lit up waiting to get into the busy harbour, which looked strange to me. If was also busy with helicopters flying people to and from the offshore oilrigs.

Forvie is a lovely nature reserve where there is a church and village buried in the sand from a storm lasting several days and abandoned in the 15th Century. It is near here that the contentious golf club belonging to Donald Trump has overtaken the area of protected machair grasses. Local people protested for years, but were overruled. The power of money won. Trump's words to describe the area that he ravaged were, "it is the most unspoilt dramatic seaside landscape in the whole world". So leave it alone, Trump!

As it was coming up to the twelfth night of Christmas, I decided to make a pagan green man for the Bongo dash-board out of moss, seaweed and bracken. It was to be a good luck charm for the van and saw out the rest of the journey with me.

I met a French woman called Claire going up the bumpy track to Rattray Head, and so I gave her a lift to the hostel where she lived. As the wind was turning to 70mph gales, I stayed there for two nights, sharing a student-type lounge with Claire and her boyfriend, Ronaldo. We put our food together and made ratatouille to celebrate her getting a job in the fish factory. The hostel was heated by a huge boiler fuelled by wooden pallets and there were many Portuguese factory workers sawing them up whilst staying there. The gales were so severe that all the trains in Scotland had stopped. With difficulty and two hoodies to keep me warm, I staggered along the deserted coast. The wind was so ferocious that Loki's ears were being blown horizontal! We went daily walks over the huge sand mountains that loom over the solitary beautiful deserted lighthouse. This was another magical place for me.

I was a little anxious about travelling in the bad weather, but after two days the sun appeared so I was off along the picturesque east coast road. On the moors, I spotted a tornado type, black wicked-looking cloud. It was miles off but coming my way. Literally two minutes later there was horizontal white out, so I stopped to shelter for a while in Aberdour. The snow soon stopped so I popped down to Pennan to see the famous post box and pub that is always shut; both appeared in the film, "Local Hero". Still anxious, I made a quick exit back up the steep lane. I sheltered the night at Macduff where I kept warm by spending part of the day at the open-air aquarium and in the evening at the closest friendly pub. There was a folk band playing there and Loki became their groupie lying at their feet being fed their unwanted chips.

The next few days, I travelled gingerly on through the snow up to Cullen. Walking was quite restricted due to the snow covering. The community centre near

Findhorn let me hook up and use their facilities, which was kind, and gave me the opportunity to look around and read about the Findhorn Community. This made interesting reading; I was most intrigued to hear about the natural spirits (devas) that helped produce the gigantic vegetables and find out about how the foundation is organised.

The Nairn Forest farm shop was one with a difference. There were no people, but a vegetable and egg vending machine in a barn. The big eggs promised double yolks and amazingly, they lived up to their reputation.

Soon the snow had turned to torrential rain so I sheltered in a "Cheese Pantry" at Ardersier and bought some cheeses and a Bongo sized mini raclette to celebrate my soon to be birthday.

I liked Inverness and spent two days there staying at the youth hostel on the outskirts of town. My shopping came to a halt when I got kicked out of the small shopping precinct by the security guard because of Loki. In the evening, I had a great night listening to both traditional Scottish folk and rock music at the

Hootenanny. As Inverness has a proper station I sorted out my train tickets for my impending trip to Wales.

Back out in the country near Cromarty I went to the "Clootie Well," another pagan site and spring where there are hundreds of pieces of material tied to the trees. They, according to legend, will bring you good health and must not be removed otherwise it brings bad health. I had no spare material so I tied up a homemade dream catcher.

I spent my birthday in Tain; a grand little town that at one time was a royal burgh. It is not very big so it only took me about half an hour to complete a tour of the town, so afterwards I went for a cold walk down the beach. Unfortunately, my birthday treats were not great. After ordering a vegetarian jalfrezi, I was given a chicken jalfrezi at the local Indian and at the Station Pub the barman could not find any wine at all, so I returned to the van a little dejected.

Tarbat Ness was where I saw my first snow plough. I expected them to become a familiar sight but it was the only one I came across. The A9 has a bridge over the

Firth, so I took it to save a few miles. At the end of the land is Dornoch, where the last woman in Scotland was executed for witchcraft. The poor woman was stripped, tarred, and put in a barrel, before being set alight. That was how they treated dementia in 1727.

In a similar vein of horridness, I passed through Golspie where there is a massive monument on the hill to the Duke of Sutherland, the aristocrat who was responsible for the 17th Century clearances. Subsequent generations have done their best to annul his bad deeds by erecting monuments at all the clearance sites in memory of the displaced people.

Past the fairy-tale looking castle at Dunrobin, I went on to Sutherland. To warm up, I had rum at the local hotel and Tom, the barman, insisted I go across the road to an "unusual bar". Always up for a challenge I went. "Captain Crabbs" is quite a strange place and you would not recognise it as a bar from the scruffy exterior. Inside it is furnished with massive wooden benches and chairs that look like they have been fettled with a chainsaw. It has strange décor and is owned by an ex soldier, Gus. He had been everywhere and done everything, but he was a good storyteller. We talked about the difficulty of secure employment up in the Highlands, his dislike of the Charity Runners on their way to John O' Groats and I listened to numerous further moans from him.

It was now near the end of January and the temperature outside was -6°. Even the locals were grizzling about the wind, so it must have been cold. I joined the A90, which can be quite a fierce road due to the intimidating log lorries, big juggernauts with flashing lights and heavy loads not 'ambling along' like me.

Helmsdale has a memorial to the victims of the clearances, a mobile bank and a stray dog that took a shine to me and followed me all around the town. Loki was not impressed. The big hotel had been closed due to a dodgy landlord serving booze and drugs to underage girls. I was very surprised that he had not been murdered by the village folk. I had a lovely gentle snowy walk in the glen and a quick swim further up at Berriedale.

Dunbeath's sole claim to fame, apart from the castle, is that it is the only place on mainland Scotland where you can see an offshore oilrig. I camped at a campsite and kept warm in the pub just down the road. The people were very friendly and the landlord of the Owl Bar told me that they literally have thousands of charity walkers and cyclists passing through the village at regular intervals, the latest being Davina McCall and her 400 cyclists. I got the impression that many local people get fed up with them.

Around the coast in this area there are many archaeological things to look at like Cairns Castle, but as the weather was so unpredictable, I only saw a few. The black mighty swirls of clouds bumping along the horizon were now a familiar and daily sight. I did manage a trip to the Whaligoe Steps; all 319 of them down to a deserted tiny turquoise coloured lagoon that was lovely and very similar to the Blue Lagoon in Wales.

The next big town of Wick seemed quite run down. As most of the houses are built with Caithness grey stone, unless the sun shines, the buildings tend to look cold and a little dismal.

I eventually reached John O' Groats and it was not snowing but bitterly cold and wet. It was not as touristy as Land's End and Loki looked a tad happier by the famous sign, but not a lot! It was Burns Night so I called in for a coffee at the Seaview Hotel, but there was nothing happening, so I moved on. Amazingly, there were no coaches or Japanese people bustling about, just Loki and I. I even had to get the girl out of the shop to take our photo. As cheap compensation I bought a postcard from her.

Dunnet Head is reached by travelling over three miles of bleak moorland, but it is the most northerly point in Britain, so I had to stay the night there. Mind, it was so windy, I had to move from near the lighthouse to a more sheltered spot. There were no signs of any bagpipes or haggis for me that Burns Night.

February 2015 – Strathy to Naast

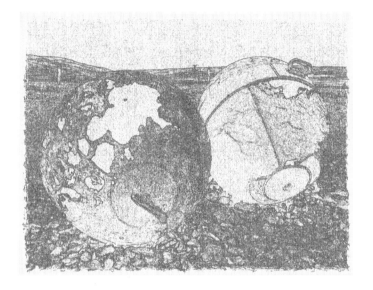

> "Travel is fatal to prejudice, bigotry and narrow mindedness"
>
> **Mark Twain**

After watching some seals at Brough Harbour, I moved onto the town of Thurso. I warmed up in a trendy music bar called Y-Not, and then went to the museum to learn all about the history of Dounreay nuclear power station and the Caithness area.

I had to return to Wales for ten days to sort out my house for re-rental and was anxious about leaving the Bongo in a safe place in Thurso. I asked a few people in the town with back-yards, but they did not want the responsibility. Next I went to the police station to see if they would house it, but they refused as they were on amber alert for potential terrorist attacks on Dounreay. Therefore, I took up the offer from the lady, Sarah, who I had met walking at Brough Harbour the day before. I took the van to her house at Dunnet where I knew it could be parked safely in her garden. I could not thank her enough. She gave me a warm bed for the night and even gave me a lift to the station in the ice, early the following morning. Such generosity!

Wales interlude

I sat back and enjoyed the long train journey of $13\frac{1}{2}$ hours from Thurso to Shrewsbury in Shropshire. There were stunning snowy scenes over the Cairngorms and Aviemore. It took me 10 days to sort out the house, so

I returned on February 10th after a 14-hour return journey; boring as it was mainly in the dark. Accepting Sarah's hospitality of another bed for the night I spent an evening talking about life in the highlands and continued my journey the next day. It was great to be back in the Bongo after couch surfing and Loki was more settled knowing where her bed was too, even if it was the size of a postage stamp.

Return to the Highlands

The tiny single track A836 with passing places was my all time favourite road of the trip. You really do feel you are in the wilderness and highlands proper.

Just past Dounreay power station is Sandside Bay, renamed by the locals, Radioactive Bay as, unsurprisingly, radioactive particles have been found there and close by is a big warning sign. I did not hang about for long. I took the tiny lane up to Strathy Point. The cliffs are very impressive and dogs are banned in case they scare the sheep over the lethal edges. They do tend to get more spooked than the Welsh sheep as they see less people. Back near the village-the locals have built a bothy type log cabin with en-suite toilet, so I stayed the night next to it, leaving a thank you letter on the pinboard the following day. Armadale is a tiny hamlet with a steep fishing bay. The fish are hauled up the cliff face with a winch and there are still old-fashioned struts for drying out the nets.

Stopping at the tiny village of Bettyhill, I went to look at the "Farr Celtic stone". Legend has it that it appeared overnight when a foreign boat was moored in the bay. It was tricky walking there due to bogs, cliffs and fences with no dog-friendly styles. I had to throw Loki over one "not very nicely". She was not pleased and looked most put out. On the road I only saw five cars today all day - it was wild, windy and wonderful. In the sea I was looking out for minke whales but unfortunately it was the wrong time of the year so I only saw white horses on the waves.

By Torrisdale, there is an "old sweep fisher" that boasts a record catch of 979 salmon in one day in 1969. This was achieved by casting a huge net across the estuary. That was one hell of a lot of fish to haul all the way home.

On local advice, I drove around the Kyle of Tongue, returning over the bridge two days later. There are only two houses along the entire stretch and camping there was so serene and peaceful. It was quite a change from the moving seascape. Not a lot happens here, proved by a plaque on the side of the road. The last significant event happened forty-eight years ago in 1967 when John and Yoko had a car crash. It must have been the influence of drugs, as not many cars pass by there to crash into. The next morning I went for a walk over the strange moss-covered rocks covering the mud flats. The weather was incredibly calm and looking out of the van door was like looking at a picture postcard. It was also strangely quiet with no birds.

Reaching the coast again, Whiten head is a towering white headland. The landscape in this area consists of craggy rocks from where you can get a good view of the uninhabited Rabbit Islands.

I imagined Tongue to be a large village, when in fact it is a tiny hamlet with two shops and two hotels. I stayed in the hamlet, as I wanted some human company and went for a drink in one of the two hotels. The barmaid,

Billie, was very chatty and informed me that she had only served two other people the whole of that day, and they had gone to bed at 8pm as they were knackered after climbing the mountain. The next day I climbed the hill to Castle Varrich, an old keep that had suffered badly in the 100-mile-an-hour gales a few weeks before, while I was on the east coast. Returning to the village, I managed to buy my weekend newspaper at the shop that was only open for one hour between 1 and 2pm on a Sunday.

I travelled around Loch Eriboll, which has an interesting prominence, Ard Neakie, almost an island jutting out into the water near Heilam. On it are the ruins of a limekiln, jetty and derelict house. As the wind was rising again I found a more sheltered spot for the night near some sheilings (a hut, common in a wild and lonely place). Only four cars passed me the following morning, commuters going somewhere to work. On the western side of the loch I came across the pottery croft of Lotte Glob. What a wonderful name. It was closed and there was no-one about, but I had a look around anyway. The place is a wonderland of weird and organic ceramic sculptures in amazing colours, obviously inspired by the landscape. I found out that Lotte Glob was a 72 year-old female ceramist; she makes some absolutely gorgeous stuff.

Next was Durness, the most north-westerly village of Britain, and a lovely place. Nearby is the hippy style Balanakeil craft village and Cocoa mountain café that sells expensive chocolate. I treated myself to the cheapest thing there, some chocolate drops that I put in the glove compartment of the van and found six months later. A solid mass melted into one and totally inedible! Back in Durness, there was a tiny local shop-cum-post office and campsite. The facilities were closed for but for £7 a night, I could hook up my van with the fan heater for warmth. I parked up on the cliff edge overlooking the now very wild sea as the gales were increasing, but I was toasty warm. I noticed that some nearby caravans were tethered down to the ground with gigantic ropes and was feeling quite vulnerable on the cliff edge with the gales gusting up to 60mph. To say I was being buffeted was an understatement and even the seagulls were swaying, it was even too blustery to take a walk. Still, I had to stay there two nights as I was waiting for a parcel from London at the tiny post office. The postmistress got all excited when I informed her that I was expecting a parcel, all the way from London. The item was vaping fluid that I had nearly run out of, so I was panicking. No shops sell it up in the highlands, and I was even told that I needed to "smoke proper" by one of the shopkeepers. Later on the first night a big "white fridge" arrived and parked up close to me. I had not had neighbours for what felt like a long time, so when I saw a bloke pass by I collared him. He was on his way to the shop to buy wine, so I asked him to get me a bottle and invited him to share it. Looking back I realised I must have appeared quite desperate or just a tart to him, but really I was just being innocently friendly. Emma and Ian were there, researching for a novel and I spent a very pleasant evening with them drinking wine, eating cheese and sharing stories and our love of Portmeirion.

The severe gales continued the following day, but I had to go for a walk somewhere and there was only Faraid Head close by. I must admit, I did not enjoy it much. It felt like an army assault course, my face was frozen and hail blasted, and I got cold and wet.

I chickened out the third night and stayed at a B&B next to the Smoo Cave Hotel. The accommodation was homely and very cute, as I found myself surrounded by all sorts of knitted, stuffed or pottery dogs. It had a comfortable bed, but sadly no bath. The owner of the establishment sensed my disappointment and suggested I go and ask for one at the hotel, as she was sure they would not mind. The barman behind the bar at the hotel thought it a very strange request. I think he was so surprised that he could not say no. The bath was so posh and clean, I was nervous about ensuring I left it spotless. I "paid" for my bath by having a pint of cider and spoke to the bar staff about how they police trouble in the highlands. It is obviously self-sorting as the nearest police officer is two hours away. The following morning I felt revived, fresh and clean and Loki was satisfied after her 3 rashers of bacon, 2 black puddings and 2 sausages breakfast. It was an exceedingly good doggie bag, which I had snaffled away. Before leaving, I wandered down to Smoo Cave in the drizzle. It is a busy tourist attraction in the summer, but that day the waterfall and cave pool were a raging torrent with the spray so fierce that I could not get anywhere near the pool.

I knew that I would be unable to reach Cape Wrath as the ferry was obviously not running in winter, but I went to look at the terminal (a tiny quay) at Keoldale. The intriguing and inaccessible mountains of Am Parbh quickly disappeared as a band of hail suddenly arrived.

Onwards to the north-western side of Scotland, I was again travelling "down" the country for the first time since Wales.

Parking at Blairmore, it was my intention to walk the four and a half miles to the most northern beach of Scotland, Sandwood Bay, but a drenching after ten minutes made me change my mind. It is a definite plan of mine to return and do the walk in fine weather. It would be great to camp there overnight on the beach with my pop up tent.

There are no villages up here, just tiny crofts, such as Polin where I walked to a remote beach through three beach gates warning of mermaids. I would describe the landscape here as "knobbly" and later, on the "geopark", changes to craggy rocks, heather, gorse and sandstone sugar loaf mountains.

Miles and miles further on I went around the next peninsular by Handa Island through Scourie, where I saw the first shop in a long time, and then on to Upper Badcall. From here, there were great views of all the islands and the Munros of Sutherland. When the cloud cleared I went on a very boggy walk to one of the inlets and came across probably the main incident of the year: a big fishing boat that had run aground. The air rescue helicopter was hovering while the lifeboat pumped water out of the sinking boat. The locals were out in force, watching with me from a tiny lane up on the hill. It all ended up fine, which was good.

The following morning I bought some eggs from a man who lived at the end of the lane. He gave me a cuppa and I did not leave for an hour. He told me all about his aches and pains and how, up to a few years ago, he raced mountain bikes, aka "Rocket Ron". He was extremely right wing and was proud of his own opinions and of his lady friend who worked 12 hour shifts in all weathers out at sea on the local salmon farm. I would have liked to meet her, but I had to move on. The couple were planning to sell up, as they were finding the extreme weather too harsh to enjoy things, which was a shame as the views from there over the Summer Isles are truly stunning, in the sun of course.

The Old Man of Stor was my next stopping place and I stayed by the lighthouse. There is a toilet, which claims to be the most remote loo in the whole of Britain. It was closed, of course, as was the "living the dream" café, but I did see dozens of wild deer. I found the "Old Man" rock a bit disappointing, as I thought he looked like a fish on its end. I got more excited about a lighthouse that I spotted, miles out on at sea which could only be on the Outer Hebrides.

Lochinver was my first town stop for a long time. I was advised to park right by the hotel and had a pleasant evening there. The barman, Phil from Leeds, was most amusing and positively rude about his starchy boss. The next day I drove off with the boot wide-open, doh! Luckily, nothing fell out otherwise there would be the entire contents of my four boxes trailing down the road. That would have been books, food, pots, pans and dog food making a clatter and hell of a mess. Phil told me of the 'wee mad road', which was my next destination. It twists and winds its way through amazing scenery, has lots of near-the-loch misses and plenty of blind summits to keep you on your toes. There was a sign for a bookshop along the way, which I got excited about but never found, it was probably barricaded up for the winter. I camped at a site at Altandhu with its turquoise sea and ate at the pub as it was still cold and windy. I had curly chips but felt a bit uneasy about them, as I am sure they were made of Smash.

My next notable stop was at Corrieshalloch Falls and Gorge. This means "ugly hollow" in Gaelic, but there is nothing ugly about it. I had to sit tight there for a good few days, as there were constant snowstorms.

Around Loch Ewe the weather improved so I could see the scenery and snow covered Munros towering in the distance. The loch was a very important military base in WW1 as it housed hundreds of boats because it is so sheltered and deep. Apparently, you could walk from one side of the loch to the other by stepping across the ships. There is lots of war memorabilia to be seen, as you might expect. I went all the way to the end of the peninsular at Cove, one of the many in Britain, stopping at a lovely red firewood beach that reminded me of India, because of the wandering cattle.

March 2015 – Badachro to Torrin (and Skye)

"I'd rather wake up in the middle of nowhere, than in any city on the earth"

Steve McQueen

My journey seems to get a bit confusing direction wise from now on, as I meandered all the way down to

Applecross and back up to catch the ferry from Ullapool to the Outer Hebrides. This was so I did not miss any of the mainland coastlines. I knew what I was doing, well most of the time anyway!

Gairloch was quite a metropolis to me, the first place in miles to cater for tourists. It has one shop, a hippy type bookshop/café, three pubs and butchers that sell vegetables. Going to Red Point (nothing there really), I stopped at Badachro and talked to the pub landlord who said it was fine to park up the night in the car park. The pub had a balcony overlooking the loch, and is situated opposite Dry Island. Dry Island is a part time island with a footbridge over to it. Its owner is an eccentric who has a spoof website of his island, "Islonia". It gained its independence recently this year and has it own flag and currency and 100% employment. You can also join online and become a virtual citizen. Mad! Back at the pub I watched Italy lose its rugby match in The Five Nations contest. The landlord was expecting crowds for the match but only had about four locals, Loki and me.

The proprietor was yet another Yorkshire man, who told me about all the yellow, no overnight camping signs all over the place. The council erected the signs two years ago, then they realised that they could not police them, so it had been a total waste of time and money. Now they cannot afford to remove them so all over in beautiful places, you see the redundant posts that I felt like angle grinding to the ground.

The weather remained cold but crisp and I had great views of the prettiest loch, Loch Maree. This lake feels quite different as it has numerous islands on it covered with pine trees. It is the only loch not used for fishing or forestry and has not been dammed. I stayed at the foot of Beinn Eighe, a stunning nature reserve and went for a walk in the woods. I returned to the van a snow woman!

Having done a long detour at last I arrived at Applecross, the highest vehicular pass in the UK with the greatest ascent. I felt in a bit of a rush to get around this famous pass in case the snow and ice increased but the road was open so I deemed it manageable. The Bongo climbed the steady uphill gradient without a struggle. There was snow by the road and the mist slowly began to envelop me. At the top severe drifts cut through the road. I could not even see the viewing place; pointless stopping, never mind camping as I had wanted. So I meandered my way down the other side for what seemed ages until the view of the valley appeared again. The hairpin bends are something else and the experience of traversing it in the snow was much more fun than going there in the summer as I had previously done, on the back of a motorbike.

I returned up north past Loch Torridon, very beautiful with the damp weather showing up a multitude of colours; rust, copper, ruby and maroon, these interspersed with bright green young Scots Pines.

Back to Gairloch for the night; it had been a busy day as I had travelled about 150 miles. Onwards to Ullapool, I travelled up Loch Broom to Badrallach to stay at an eco campsite, but it was closed of course. At the end of the track is the walk to Scoraig, a tiny settlement with no electricity or cars, which unfortunately I did not have time to walk to.

On the moors near Loch Broom, I camped in some woods and came across Alistair, the local gamekeeper looking after his charges…six hundred deer. He told me about his work with them and the wild goats roaming around the van. I named that place in the middle of nowhere, "Broken Bridge" as the nearby wooden footbridge was in a sad way. There had been so much rain recently that the next part of the trip was a plethora of waterfalls, large, small, narrow, wide, but always one thing in common: Fast and furious.

At last, I arrived at Ullapool to catch the ferry across to the Outer Hebrides. Ullapool remains quaint, but they are building a big terminal now, whereas before, it was a tiny port-a-cabin. Due to severe gales, the last few ferries had been cancelled, but the captain's decision was to sail that day, so great! I was so excited, as I love the Scottish ferries.

My journey over the next four months in Scotland was mainly island hopping, returning to bits of the mainland, that I had not covered.

The Outer Hebrides

Harris and Lewis

K was now joining me for a few days and we arrived late on the island, so stayed the first night in a B&B in Stornoway. Unfortunately, it was like a nursing home but happily it did not smell of wee!

The next day we went to the north of the island, Tolsta and Ness, both in a snowstorm. It was very grey and deserted and everyone was at church; it felt like a very religious area. More interesting are the Calanais Standing stones. I think these are the best in the UK, not for their location, but their stunning shape and texture.

The next stop was my inspirational beach, Ardroil by Uig sands. I had been there a few years ago and discovered this isolated beautiful beach in the summer sunshine with a port-a-loo and £1 per night camping sign. I vowed to return on my trip. Yes, it was different now. There is a stack of toilets and the wind was gusting at 90mph. We found the farmer, paid our fee of now £7 a night, and sheltered from the gales behind the dunes. I have never experienced wind like it, and I was literally blown over outside. Even inside, downstairs on the rock and roll bed, we were ferociously buffeted and swaying in the wind. It is still, one of my favourite places though.

Another unusual place nearby is Bosta, with its jellybean Iron Age house and a tide and time bell on the beach.

After a few days, I returned to Stornaway to return K to London. All the boats had been cancelled due to the inclement weather, so he had to fly back home and I was away on my own again.

Located in the spectacular Harris Hills is the Eagle Observatory where I stayed for a few hours watching three golden eagles. What amazing creatures they are. It is mesmerising just watching them hovering around the untouchable mountains. Back on the road the Gaelic names around here were stumping me, as I do not know how to pronounce them.

The furthest southwest peninsular is the end of the road at Huisinis, a small hamlet with two beaches. It was so gorgeous here; I stayed one night on each beach. Scarp Island is close by and whilst walking I met a couple, Jill and Donald McKenzie, who ended up having a warming cuppa in the van and who had an interesting story to tell. Donald lived on the island as a child with his family until 1971, and they were the last residents to leave. The island is a huge rock with very little shelter, so there were only a few people, sheep and cattle in the island. He told me how his family would herd the cattle to swim from the island across the tempestuous sea, followed by an incredibly steep and dangerous mountain path to Huisinis. On the island, according to Donald, the resident teachers for the few children there would only last a year, their romantic notion soon shattered by the harsh winters. The island is also famous for a German who invented an unsuccessful rocket for the post! Lastly, twins from Scarp made the Guinness Book of Records. They were born 40 miles apart (one in Inverness and the other on Scarp) and 40 hours apart. Incredibly both twins and mother survived. The owner of the island now, according to Donald, is a very caring and loyal man who is building a distillery in Tarbet to provide the local employment.

Whilst there, I could not resist a quick dip in the turquoise sea and on one of my walks saw a very faint St Kilda from the headland. I only saw four visitors all weekend. It was great as I felt I was a part of the island, like the animals and birds around.

Further south overlooking Taransay Island is Luskentyre a sparse settlement adjacent to a vast sandy beach and estuary. In the lay-bys, you are invited to wild camp and £5 goes to the Harris Trust to upkeep its beauty. What a wonderful place.

In the evening, I was just about to settle down for the night when I noticed strange lights in the sky. I can only describe it as gigantic white torches flashing on and off in all directions spanning the whole of the sky. I lay down on a nearby picnic bench with a hot water bottle and blanket for 3 hours watching them. It was brilliant a monochrome version of what I guessed was the Northern Lights. My feet were still cold in the morning, but it was worth it. Just a shame I was on my own as Loki did not appreciate the show.

Moving on, I passed numerous beautiful beaches and went on windy walks until I reached Leverburgh where I stocked up with food. I had not seen a shop in three days, never mind people to talk to. Here, I caught the ferry over to Berneray Island.

Berneray Island

The crossing was calm and bright so I could see all the islets and lovely sheep on rocks everywhere. It was wall to wall dunes and beaches. I met a couple in their 90s who had moved here a year ago. They told me how they had spent 12 years on the road previously. That put my mini adventure into perspective. I stayed the night by a thatched cottage that I only found out later was one of the three Hebridean youth hotels.

North Uist, Benbecula and South Uist

It was pretty barren on Benbecula, but I went for a walk into the only forest on the island. It was so refreshing to see trees again. I stayed the next two nights at

Howmore Hostel, South Uist. It is a beautiful thatched cottage with a real fire. So there I was on my own, lugging bags of coal from the bottom of the garden to keep the fire going. The beach here is usually sandy, but due to the storms, it was covered in seaweed. The smell was so pungent that I felt quite nauseous and had to return over the cliffs. I explored the collection of medieval chapels by the hostel and walked in the dunes and machair grass. During my stay, there was a total eclipse of the sun happening. I was so excited I woke up at 6am and prepared my pinhole paper and binoculars. Come the vital time, at 9.30am, the rain clouds washed away any hope. It did become eerily dark and quiet, not pitch black, but dark like at dusk, similar to a very dark stormy day, typical of a Scottish winter. However, come 9.45am, the clouds cleared and I did see the eclipse, like a crescent moon for a few minutes, it was awesome! I had no one to share the experience with me, so I left a postcard about it in the hostel for future travellers to read.

Barra Island

The next day, I caught the ferry over to Barra. I went as a foot passenger as getting the van over was very expensive. I assumed that a bus would arrive at the Barra terminal to go into town, but I was wrong. There was no public transport in sight, so I scrounged a lift from a deliveryman who took me to Castlebay. A quick walk and look around the town was all I had time for. The Yorkshire couple at the post office kindly sorted me a return bus to the ferry. It is a request bus, which you have to ask for with three hours notice. They also told me of the "Barra Bidet". This is when the wind and pressure of water is such that the contents of your toilet are spewed up onto your bathroom floor. Apparently, it does not happen often, but when it does, it is a bit surprising as you get no warning and makes a right mess!

Returning up north to Lochmaddy took a while as it is 47 miles of very small roads, but that was where I was catching the ferry over to Skye. It was a bit of a rough crossing and when I took Loki up on deck, she got her "belly legs" on. This is where she crouches down low in order to shorten her legs, a most comical sight to witness. She does this on swinging bridges too!

Isle of Skye

Arriving at Uig, I went north first to Duntulm Castle for the night. I really appreciated the beautiful scenery: grassland, mountains and hobbit hills. The variety really made this trip worthwhile. I even began to get bored with stunning beaches if they lacked variety. Back at the castle ruins the wind almost took the van door off and sent me over the castle cliff into the sea, but it was a lovely peaceful place to spend the night.

Next, in the Trotternish area of Skye, at Staffin, I managed to get the van stuck in mud. Luckily a local pulled me out and refused any money for the help. It was quite embarrassing as it was Sunday afternoon. A local lady phoned her cousin and he and his friend arrived in what I would call a Jeremy Clarkson jeep. It was a huge 4x4 complete with headlights on top, in fact, way over the top, but I mustn't grumble. Prior to that, I searched for the dinosaur footprints on the beach, unsuccessfully.

The next day, was exactly one year since I had set out from Portmeirion. Plan A was to celebrate with a meal out, but there were no hotels nearby. Plan B was to have a mini bottle of champagne, but there were no shops. Therefore, it was Plan C: salad and a glass of wine in the van. The roof stayed down that night as the weather was similar to the night I set off in Wales. It was a time to pause and reflect about all the wonderful experiences I had over the last year. In the morning whilst having my coffee, an otter crossed right in front of the van, scurrying away in the rain.

The houses on Skye are mainly painted white, which is much more cheerful than the grey Hebridean dwellings. Wind and torrential rain prevailed, but I did manage to catch a bit of sunshine on my walks in-between showers. I was now in "Lord of the Rings" country with its pinnacles, precipices and pillars of the Trotternish. I met a couple who had camped out the previous night in a tiny tent in the gales and rain. They were walking across the island and seemed unperturbed by the weather.

The Quiraing is one of Scotland's most popular destinations so I was not surprised to meet up with "crowds". For me, that was a gathering of more than six people. I had had all the beautiful places to myself up to now and felt quite reluctant to share them. Now I had to deal with a crowd of Japanese tourists. These students were all making a fuss of Loki which she did not mind but became all embarrassed when they included her in their selfies. It was a clear day by now and I had fantastic views over Raasay, Applecross and even Red Point. I climbed up the Old Man of Storr; this is worthwhile even if you end up with jelly legs due to the steep climb.

At Portree I took a short sea eagle-spotting boat trip. I felt I was a part of a Monty Python sketch when the skipper produced a fish, waved it about a bit then threw it in the sea to encourage the eagle to visit us. A seagull immediately went for it then flew off rapidly following by the huge swoop of a sea eagle that snatched it and was away. It happened so quickly that some people on the boat missed it. The eagle's size close up is amazing.

I did some laundry at the hostel in Portree where I met a man who claimed he had walked all the way from London in one month. Possibly, but always wondered what route he took. Anyway, I kindly gave him the rest of my hot air to dry his clothes. That night I rough parked with great views overlooking Raasay Island and the mountains. I was treated to a small display of fireworks, close by at midnight, but never found out what the celebration was about. There must be something nutritious in fireworks, as in the morning, a crowd of sheep and gulls were gathering and having a feast on the site.

Raasay Island

I drove on all the roads here. This is no great feat as there are only three roads on the island. I saw the Pictish stones, an old chapel and went to the end of Callum's Road. This road was built by Callum, a resident in the 1960s. It took him 10 years to complete, as the council had refused to extend it to his abode. It is very steep and windy, wandering its way through the rough and rugged rock-scape. It is an impressive feat of personal engineering and hard work. I stayed by the derelict castle and in the morning and woke up in the mist and as it cleared, the flat-topped volcanic mountain appeared covered in a heavy frost. The sheep outside were eating their high-energy food that looked like treacle in big red tubs. It seems they get lots of nourishment from this, as they seem to spend more time contemplating their future and admiring the scenery than grazing, unlike the Welsh sheep.

I took a day visit back onto the mainland, to Eilean Donan Castle. It has an impressive restoration history and is exactly what a castle should be, full of tiny stairs, corridors and spy holes.

Back on the Skye Vaternish peninsular, at Trumpan, there is a ruined chapel with a grim history. In 1578, clan retribution resulted in the whole congregation being locked inside the chapel and the thatched roof set on fire, burning the whole congregation. Only one young girl managed to escape. I ended up staying at Dunvegan and noticed the first daffodils appearing. Many had been damaged by the recent winds, so I adopted them for the Bongo which looked very homely. The lambs had not arrived yet as the sheep were still waddling around heavily pregnant; but spring was on the way. Nearby is an unusual beach at Claigan. This isolated beach is totally made up of seaweed coral.

Glenbrittle near the Black Cuillin Mountains is full of human tortoises (hill walkers) and bearded men driving fun buses. I stayed in a beautiful valley but the mountains were shrouded in mist and I was unable to reach the Fairy Pools as the river crossing was a raging torrent. Instead, I discovered a pub at Carbost with an attached bunkhouse so I stayed the night there. The dormitory had a fantastic loch view and it felt like staying in a 4-star hotel. The pub was very friendly and the team that worked there all mucked in together, cooking, cleaning, serving - no hierarchy, which seemed great. I was offered a ticket to the Portree Music Festival by Scott, a bearded local. No good as I would have moved on by then.

I got talking to Lindsay, the barmaid about my lights in the sky on Lewis and she thought they were fireballs, not the Northern Lights. I shared by bedroom with three German hill walkers, Gunter, Greta and Gespa. Gunter jumped down off his bunk bed in the morning like a gazelle, obviously trying to impress his lady friends. I gave them all a lift to the Fairy Pools and then bumped into them at the pub at Sligachan. I joked with them that despite the rucksacks, they are only going on a pub-crawl, not hill walking at all. I had gone for a stiff rum at the pub for a very good reason. To celebrate being alive and to calm myself down. Why? Because, I nearly drowned in the Fairy Pools!

The raging torrent of yesterday had reduced so the valley river was crossable. Everyone raves about this renowned wild swimming place so I went to have a look. On the way I met Howard, a brazen bloke carrying a wet suit, who informed me he was going for a swim. That was it, he had exposed my competitive streak so I had to go for a dip. I walked all the way back to the van for my swimming gear - a flouncy red jump suit type thing. As I got to the pool, it started sleeting and Howard was nowhere to be seen, but my mind was made up. I do not like to make a spectacle of myself, so I waited until some walkers were out of sight, then I eased my way down into one of the several plunge pools. I could not feel the bottom and it was very cold, but beautiful, so I swam over to the little rock ledge to the further pool where the waterfall was cascading down. My idea was just to touch the far wall and get out as I knew that even in summer, these pools are icy cold. I did touch the wall, but instead of getting back to the ledge, I got sucked under the water like in a washing machine. I managed to get to the surface to gasp for air and got sucked under again. This happened five times before I managed to pull myself back to safety by pushing with all my might from the rock face. I used all my strength and willpower to do this. My mind had gone into overdrive, *you must survive,* and I pictured my body floating on the pool, dead. I had tried to cry for help, but no one was around and you could not hear me anyway due to the sound of the waterfall. I also knew that I would die of hypothermia if I stayed in the icy water too long. Relieved, I sat on the rock ledge for a good few minutes to get my breath back, I did not even feel cold; I think I was in shock. Loki was looking down at me from the top, totally oblivious to what had just happened. She had the look of "been for your swim, can we go now". Five minutes later, a lady arrived and said "good on you" for going in. I replied,

"No, bloody stupid, I nearly drowned". Therefore, my safety motto now is: DO NOT go swimming in any mountain rivers in winter after torrential rain. I met Howard back at the car park later and he had chickened out - sensible fellow.

I was quiet and thoughtful for the rest of the day and had a lovely wild camp evening in the forest near Torrin. I went for a walk up the Blue Mountain, but sensibly turned back when it started snowing. I was aware how the Scottish weather can change within minutes and I did not want another near death experience for quite a while.

Heading for the ferry off Skye, I made my way to Armadale. The boat was on amber alert due to the gales, but I made it onto my next destination Mallaig, back on the mainland.

I moved on for the night to Traigh, a deserted golden beach near the golf course. The old Road skirts around numerous sandy coves and rocky outlets. I went to Camusdarach beach where the film "Local Hero" was shot, yet another beautiful sandy cove, then a long drive past Glenuig to Ardtoe. I remember this place as it has a huge "monster midge" painted on a rock by the side of the road. A local artist with a sense of humour obviously created it.

April 2015 - Fort William to Creagan (and Mull)

"If you think adventure is dangerous; try routine"

Paulo Coelho

Leaving the coast and going inland for a few days with K again. On the way, I called at Claggan Museum of Treasure, full of gems, fossils and crystals and had lunch in the van before going up to Fort William and onto beautiful Glen Coe. It had taken K two days to drive up on the motorbike from London, but we had a great time at Red Squirrel campsite and ate at the Clachan Inn, full of walkers.

The next day, the fantastic walk up Glen Nevis was in sunshine when we walked over the cable bridge. Loki obviously had to swim across the river to stay with us, and in the evening we met a Scandinavian man called Loki and his name was even spelt the same way!

We explored the Ardnamurchan peninsular, staying near the lighthouse and Sanna Point. It was very peaceful and quiet probably as it was so cold and windy still.

Isle of Mull

K left me at colourful Tobermory. Billie Bongo was also in need of repairs to the steering and brakes, so I had to hang around for a good few days on Mull whilst spare parts arrived from London. A bit of a déjà vu, as I had been stuck on Mull 20 years ago waiting for Harley Davidson parts. Consequently I spent the next few days in Salen where the garage was and Tobermory where I did a couple of nights B&B. The owners were a friendly couple and they even dog sat for me in the evenings. My entertainment came from the brilliant mobile cinema, the Screen Machine, which travels around all the western Isles. I went to see all the three available films. "Shaun the Sheep", I shared with small children and grandparents. "Fifty Shades of Grey" with drunken, crassly dressed young women (not a single man in sight!) and lastly, "The Theory of Everything" surrounded by normal people. A sudden hailstorm on the tin roof was deafening. During the day, I walked both ways from the town; to the lighthouse one way for a cold picnic, then towards Aros Park, which is very secluded.

I managed a couple of nights at Calgary before the major repairs were due. There is an official wild campsite here next to the river, but there were not many people there, so I had a fire by the beach all on my own. It is a good swimming beach and the sculpture park is worth a visit too. On the second day I was walking along the beach, when I heard music permeating through the dunes. I went to explore and discovered a live band "Macanta" performing in the dunes. There were a lot of them playing, one vocalist being backed by variety of instruments: harp, viola, mandolin, cello, guitars and drums. It sounded good, so I was looking forward to some free afternoons entertainment, but they were playing the same song over and over and over again, so I soon got bored. It was a promotional video for Calmac ferries.

Back at Salen and I had to hang around a bit longer for the van to be fixed, so went on a local walk in the wood. Sounds idyllic, but there were fences everywhere and Loki and I ended up literally in a bog, me over my wellies and Loki submerged twice. We were washed off in the rain and I went for a coffee in the hotel to dry out.

The Spanish waitress was lovely and gave me a towel to dry off. Meanwhile, Loki shook herself off against the white walls. I did offer to clean it, but the staff were fine about it. They are obviously used to muddy walkers. I popped over to Ulva Island on the tiny ferry and looked at the basalt columns and Eas Fors, another wild swimming waterfall that eventually tumbles over a steep cliff into the sea.

Staffa Island

Nothing prepares you for how wonderful this island is. Fingal's Cave, with huge basalt columns is awesome. It is literally hard to tear yourself away. There were about 100 puffins lolling about on the water by the boat. It was the first time I had seen a puffin, so I had a dilemma. Do I go see the puffins on land, or the cave, as time was limited. I tried to do both, but did not wait long enough for the puffins. I learned that the puffins tend to go on land if people are present, as they feel protected from the bigger predatory sea birds. This is why people are able to get up close and take terrific photos of them. On the return boat, my neighbour had a close up photo of one and said he had to pay his wife to not stay on the island with the puffins as they were so cute. The cave was equally as mesmerising with the waves crashing ferociously against the vertical stacks.

After about a week, my van repair was complete, so I drove to the south of Mull. Ronnie the garage owner had done a great job, and so was able to have a good few whiskies at my expense as I drove off £600 lighter.

Far South West of Mull just outside the village of Fionnphort, Fidden Farm was so gorgeous that I stayed a record three nights. I went numerous swims in this stunning location, and I was surrounded by beautiful sunsets and sunrises. The only disaster was my second best friend (after Loki) burst. My hot water bottle exploded, luckily, under my feet and not in bed. I walked to tiny Erraid Island, where Robert Louis Stevenson set part of "Kidnapped", and spent a day on the island of Iona trying to avoid the religious bits. It was there that I saw and smelt the first garlic flowers of the season. This was quite poignant for me as it reminded me of the beginning of my journey in Wales. The campsite at Fidden is convenient for walking and exploring the deserted beaches and a view overlooking Iona and numerous islets. Apart from the panorama, I had my own tiny beach to swim in. The landscape reminded me of the inside of the Pink Floyd album cover of "Wish You Were Here" which I thought was very apt.

To the south of the headland, Uisken is a tiny hamlet where wild camping is encouraged on the croft with permission from the crofter. Further on is Carsaig where there is a hermits cave complete with windows, I stayed the night by Ben More on the side of Loch Scridain and the following day, looked at the weavers in Ardalanish. It is an impressive set up, as all the weaving is done on restored Victorian looms. I saw the noisy machines working and experienced their deafening sound. When observing them, you are advised to stand in a certain position, as it has been known for the shuttles to fly off the machine and take out your kidney.

Lochbuie is a tiny place down an eight-mile rickety track that takes you past lakes and big pine forests. Again, wild camping is allowed, so I joined a 70-year-old Australian lady called Shirley camping. We shared a glass of wine in the evening, but she retired to bed at about 8pm. She was quite a character as she wanted, like me, to go to all the remotest places and she had even hired a boat to take her to uninhabited shores, weather permitting that is. By the hamlet I went on a long walk across the bay to look at the mausoleum and nearby stone circle. By the beach is a shed/post office selling local goods, so I bought some eggs. It is unmanned and you pay by the honesty box, but I did meet a woman the next morning. She was stocking up the shop with her homemade cakes before taking her daughter on the sixteen mile school run.

On 23rd April, I returned to Tobermory to attend the four-day Mull Music Festival. All the pubs and hotels had music on all day and night so I had a great time taking it all in. There was quite a variety of music from traditional Scottish pipes and fiddles to violins, harps and rock bands. It was easy to meet up with people so I teamed up with Sue from Manchester, Mike and Jenny from Kendal and some "rufty- tufty" divers from somewhere down south. They had nicked a huge "Vote Cameron" banner as a joke and put it above their bus. The whole of the harbour car park was full of mobile homes and campervans. I got to know my immediate neighbours, Barbara and Duncan from the Cairngorms and Trudy and Jim from the Island of

Tiree. Amazingly, the weather was sunny and warmish so we shared gin and tonics outside and even had a fish supper washed down with cava down by the harbour. They were all good fun and I had a three-day party with them.

I had spent three weeks on Mull and I almost felt I lived there. It is not as spectacular as Skye, but more cuddly and laid back, which I like. I wanted to explore the Morven peninsular so I crossed back to the mainland from Fishnish to Lochaline. I turned left up the solitary road, right to the end at Drimnin. At the side of the road is an interesting stone with a big hole, it is thought to be a wishing stone and an ancient boundary between the Gaelic and Pictish tribes. I crossed Loch Linnhe on the ferry at Corran (for the third time).

I stayed at Keil, a deserted shingle bay then onto the Appin area, which is quite wooded, pretty and gentle. This landscape is the total opposite to the other side of the loch where I was the previous night; wild bare and mountainous. I stopped with all the other tourists to take a photo of Castle Stalker on it little island and then got lost and ended up down a tiny lane at "Bongoland". This was a house name plaque with a magician's hat on it. I got out of the van to take a photo just as the owner an elderly man, came out of the front door. The story goes that Bongo is his nickname, but I still do not know what significance the fez has, or if it is in any way, connected to the famous 1960s magician, Ali Bongo.

May 2015– Oban to Ardlussa (Jura) (and Arran and Mull)

"No matter where you go, there you are"

Buckeroo Banzai

From Appin I took the foot ferry to Lismore Island and walked to Port Ramsay. It is intriguing how the landscapes around Loch Linnhe are so different. The

Appin side is gentle and leafy whilst the other side is rugged, rocky and mountainous moorland. Tiny Eriska Island is a private five star hotel and spa accessed by a noisy slatted wooden bridge. I went to look, ignoring all the "residents only" signs. It looked austere and snotty, so I moved on. While the sun shone I took an afternoon walk along a local beach with a very jolly name, Tralee.

K joined me again and we met up in Oban. It felt very strange camping on a site where I could hear the neighbours. Our first destination the next day was the Slate Islands. The Atlantic Bridge takes you on to Seil Island and Easdale. The village is full of single storey workers cottages and the old quarries are full up with water. We went for a drink in the pub in the evening, but, as we were the only punters, were asked to leave at 9.30pm because the proprietor wanted to shut up early and go to bed. Easdale is also famous for its annual World Championship Stone Skimming contest.

Next, we went round the Kilmartin area. This area is a dream if you like ancient relics. There are castles, cairns, stone circles and cup and ring markings on certain rocks all within walking distance of each other.

We continued making our way down to the west coast of Kintyre, staying at a campsite in the tiny hamlet of Tayvallich. Seems it is a Christian site, as women were wandering about clutching bibles and there was hymns being sung in the hall. I wondered what they thought of my pagan Patmobile. However, the views over Knapdale and Jura were stunning. K then returned home, so I took a long drive around the loch and back to the coast where I caught the first ferry of the day from Tayinloan to Gigha Island. It was only 8 am and so I passed the school kids getting off the ferry to go to school on the mainland. On the island, Mr Horlicks, of the night time drink, planted Archamore Gardens. It is a rambling and mysterious place, full of hidden corners and paths surrounded by colourful azalea and rhododendron bushes.

This part of the west coast is pretty wild and rugged. You often see odd singular old caravans sited right by the wild cliffs, adorned with tiny gardens and fences around. I wondered if they have squatters' rights to be there. In comparison, the next place I stopped for the night was at West Point. This is a beautiful sandy bay of several miles with a backdrop of dunes. I thought that I had found a very rare sea bean on the beach washed up all the way from the Caribbean, but it was really a piece of seaweed in the shape of a broad bean.

I passed across the Kintyre peninsular to Campbeltown with its rocket church spire and awful sculpture of Linda McCartney in her memorial garden. Old Campbeltown is overshadowed by Davaar Island, which is quite beautiful. One side is male like, with rough steep rugged rocks and the other side is female with gentle rounded, smooth moorland. On to Machrinhanish that was full of golfers, so I made a quick retreat to Keil point where I went to view the well and footprints carved in the rocks. These are all associated with the legend that St Columba who landed there in 564 AD. The nearby Keil caves were inhabited at various times ranging from prehistoric times right up to 1881.

Kintyre is very lush and green until you reach the seven mile road to the end of the Mull over moorland. You pass through farm gates that have open styles at the side with steps. This seems like easy access for intelligent sheep I thought. It was a one mile steep walk down to the lighthouse, but not worth it in the strong winds and rain. Even my glasses blew out of the van and down the lane. I had the song, "Mull of Kintyre", constantly rattling around in my head, which was annoying, so I renamed the tune "Desolate Point". It does not have the same ring about it for a cheesy song title but an apt name for the place that day.

Travelling down the east coast the road with hairpin bends and wooded valleys took me to Torridsdale. I stayed near the private castle and beach then I moved on to catch the ferry from Claonaig to Lochranza on Arran.

Arran Island

At the Cock of Arran in the north, I went in search of "Huttons Unconformity" (a geological thing). The rocks had been laid down at right angles to each other, but the Unconformity is very obscure and difficult to spot. On the roadside going back was a very young deer eating a house's compost. He was so into it that I managed to get within a foot of him to get a close up photo of his green, grassy nose. I parked up at Sannox picnic site next to a river. This was handy, as I had literally gone up to my knees in a bog on my last walk where a 4x4 had gone up to the axle. So I washed myself and my clothes, the old fashioned way, in the river.

Across the island at Lamlash, you get a great view of Holy Isle from an old cairn at the Giant's Cave at the top of the mountain. Buddhist Monks own Holy Isle, but I was informed that you could only walk on certain parts of the island. This grated on my own "Freedom to Roam" belief so I gave the trip over there a miss especially as the weather was not great that day.

Going south at Whiting Bay, there is a lovely village shop that does terrific pasties. I stayed at a campsite at Kildonan next to the hotel. I was hoping for a lively evening as a dozen bikers arrived, but by the time I got to the bar, they had gone to bed (9.30pm!). The hotel overlooks Pladda Island and the towering Ailsa Craig in the distance.

Passing through Kilmory, I called in at the Creamery and bought myself some cheese. Not any old cheese but one that was voted the best in the whole world in 2013. I spent the rest of the day looking at rocks. The Machrie Moor standing stones look pretty amazing. There are several circles on the moor and some of them incredibly tall. Further north, I took a walk up to the glacial loch of Coire Fhionn. It is a bit of a trek, but worth it for the views. I was greeted at the top of the mountain by a ferocious hailstorm and there are no trees for shelter. Also caught out was a young couple. This was an amusing sight as he was trying to shield her from the gales and hail with his coats, like a matador. She only had a flimsy dress on and had very blue knees. Even Loki was hiding behind me as the hail was pricking her. That evening, I parked up by the lonesome white beach shed. This old shed is quite the celebrity of the island, well photographed due to both its character and desolate location. This part of the island was my favourite, as it is wilder with tiny hamlets spread out along the shores. The following morning, I heard a cuckoo - it must be spring officially now- so I caught the ferry back to Kintyre and stayed the night at

Tarbet, a warm and friendly town. I found out that there was to be a Viking festival in the next few days with longboats traversing the lochs. The lady at the information place seemed very put out when I suggested they should burn the boats as a grand finale to make the festival more authentic.

Islay Island

Islay, to be honest, is pretty boring and flat compared to the other islands; however, I was arriving in time for the Whisky and Music festival, so at least it was lively. Unfortunately, I hate whisky, but that probably was a good thing. K was joining me for a few days. Not as a rufty-tufty biker this time, but a posh person flying in to the cute and tiny airport. We stayed at Kintra campsite four miles from anywhere and in the dunes overlooking Laggan Bay. This is a remote surfing beach, but also the dunes are full of hares. We explored the only mountainous bit of the island at the Mull of Oa where there is a huge American Monument memorial to the men who lost their lives in two shipwrecks off Islay in 1918. In addition, there is a big Celtic cross at Kildalton and nearby there was tea in a flask and cakes by the side of the road with an honesty box. Lastly, we went to Finlaggan ruins on an islet that was once the seat of the Lord of the Isles. Islay has numerous distilleries and as it was the festival, you could camp overnight outside any of them. So I had a social life for a few days, live music at the Lagavulin distillery and a Ceilidh at Port Ellen. Amazingly, I managed to avoid dancing too, which was good. We met up with two yachtsmen who had sailed over from Ireland. A lively pair soused on whisky and in the morning, we were awoken by the dulcet sound of bagpipes beckoning the punters to buy more whisky. The last place I went with K before returning him to the airport was the singing sands, Traigh Bhan near Port Ellen. I tried to get them to sing, but they remained silent. I even asked a group of small children if they had heard them sing and they just looked at me as if I was mad.

I returned to the Lagavulin distillery for their open day and 200-year celebration. For part of the celebration, the distillery had a huge cake and a lady sang "Happy Birthday," which went down like a lead balloon! That evening, I went to a folk concert in the hall, but unfortunately, it was like "Islay's got Talent," Ok if you like that sort of thing.

I travelled onto the next leg of Islay to Bruichladdich distillery to do a "fair dos" for myself and buy a bottle of the fantastic botanical gin. This really is unusual, made with 22 botanicals all from Islay. One word of advice, do not have tonic with it, it is beautiful on its own over lots of ice and a slice of fresh lime. My stop for the night was at the south-westerly tip of the island between Portnahaven and Port Wemyss, a pretty horseshoe village overlooking Orsay Island. There is a great old pub there called "An Tigh Seinnse". I tried to find out what this name meant, but no one seemed to know. Later I discovered that it is Gaelic for "house of singing". Anyway, I had a great evening there listening to a blues band called Bluewater. It is a tiny pub and it was stuffed full, so I sat half the night wedged against the wall on a pretty uncomfortable coal scuttle. Later I managed to get a seat next to sprightly 79 year old, Wendy (She told me her age three times!). She was a smiley lady with a cheeky girlish face and was enjoying the music as much as the rest of us.

I had a late start the next day when I went to see a derelict wave generator. It was a huge concrete building built at great expense, but had never been used. Returning to the van, I spotted a ferret or stoat scuttling in front of me. It was running too quickly to know which it was.

Arriving at Port Charlotte, the sun came out so I couldn't resist a quick swim as I had not had one for a good few days. My stop for the night was at Machir Bay, a big expansive sandy beach complete with a sunken shipwreck. It was a bit busy there; I counted 12 people on the beach, but did get talking to my neighbours, Bruno, Jim and son, Tom. They were from Leeds and travelling in a converted ambulance. This was very apt as Bruno had broken her leg.

At the far north-west of the island is Sanaigmore, not very pretty, but nice and remote. Quite rightly, I got told off by a farmer who came screaming up on his quad bike, as his cows were calving. I did see the sign, but misread it as a beware of the bull sign. So I left pretty sharpish and very embarrassed. There is a very sad memorial here for 241 people lost at sea in 1847.

They were mainly women and children, Irish immigrants escaping the potato famine. My last walk of the day was to Ardnave Point; lovely, wild and with deserted beaches, but it took up the rest of the day as I had to keep diverting due to more cows in calf.

My last night in Islay was at Bunnahabhain overlooking the Paps of Jura. Whatever man named these magnificent grey slate mountains that, I decided, was a sexually frustrated drunk who had not seen, never mind been with a woman for at least twenty five years. Why? Because they look nothing like any breasts, young, old, big or small. They have no nipples, are lumpy and there are three of them! I rest my case.

June 2015 – Craighouse (Jura) to Port Carlisle (and Bute)

> *"Let your memory be your travel bag"*
>
> **Alexander Solzhenitsyn**

Jura

This was my favourite island of the whole trip due to its remoteness and inaccessibility and the magnificent paps, of course. There is only one way to get to Jura and that is via the 10-minute ferry from Port Arskaig on Islay. It's a small ferry, too small to take big motor homes, so I liked it even more for that. I parked near the ferry terminal at Feolin and took a walk up the forestry track going north. Past a single house, lighthouse and small loch, there was a sign for "The quagmire of the black beast and giant witch" path, which spooked me a little, but I carried on past the raised beach, rock stacks on the coast and close up views of the towering impressive silver grey quartz mountains on the other side. I had to wade through knee high bogs to avoid the cows again and Loki (bog dog) was covered. She went for an involuntary swim in the river on the way back; otherwise, the Bongo would have become very smelly and dank.

After four hours I returned to the van to travel eight miles to the only real village, Craighouse. It is a great village with a small distillery, hotel, tearoom, shop, school and village hall. There was a craft exhibition there, so I had a look around and spoke to the photographer who had some prints of the Northern Lights taken from Jura. He confirmed the date of his photos, March 19th, the same night as I saw the "lights" on Lewis. Therefore, I deduced that what I saw on the same night were the Northern Lights and not fireballs! I was chuffed about that.

I parked up by the pier, and was able to use the camping facilities from the hotel. I had a well-needed shower, but my bog feet were engraved with oily bog stuff, so a scrub in the van was the only thing to get clean. Unfortunately, the washing machine was broken but I got the barman, Kyle, to do my washing. He later informed me that he only did my laundry as he thought I was a practising witch. He had spotted my pentagon on the van and he also thought that my pebble necklace was a powerful witch's charm! He was most disappointed to find out I was not a real witch, but we had a good chat anyway. Well, he did the chatting whilst his lovely Goth girlfriend and I listened.

In the morning, I drove north up the only road of the island past the hamlets of Lagg and Tarbert. Ardlussa is a lush patch with a mansion in it, but then the road traversed three miles of moorland on a bumpy track. I parked at the end of the public road to walk the four miles to Brownhills. This is the cottage where George Orwell wrote his renowned book "1984". The track resembles something out of a children's story book; a path meandering around the moor up and down and round and round as far as the eye could see. Brownhills Cottage is a substantial size and has been maintained well. George Orwell, or Eric Blair, as the locals knew him, really had wanted to get away from the people and live in solitude in order to write the book. It was a pity that he was ill much of that time. Having had a snoop around, I made my way back to the van. Luckily, it was sunny most of the return walk, but I did get caught out in two hail storms. That was ok, as the wind and sun soon dried me off. A few miles past Brownhills at the far north of Jura is the spectacular Corryvrechan Whirlpool. It is reported to be the third largest whirlpool on the planet. It is not visible through binoculars off the mainland, but you can get boats trips around it. On my walk back I met a landowner going to check on the cottage. I called her Lady Ardlussa (as she lived at the mansion). Her father knew Eric and she said he had seemed very depressed, but a real character. She gave me permission to stay the night at the end of the road on her estate and assured me that I would not be disturbed. Sadly she did not invite me back for canapés and a wee dram, which was a bit disappointing as I would have loved to have talked with her longer about the local history, but she seemed in a hurry. It was quite an eerie evening, and night, being on my own on the moors, which were enveloped in wind and rain, but it was wonderful. Not a soul disturbed me and the only company I had were two very tiny birds. I returned that evening to the hotel to have a lovely warm meal and some company. I had another "small world" incident as John sat next to me and informed me that his wife went to my grammar school in Stockport, my birthplace. In addition, German John told me how every year he dresses up in his leathers to attend the big motorbike event at the Ace Café in London. There, he meets up with another hundred or so bikers to ride down to Brighton as pretend Hell's Angels. I guess it's like a mock battle between the Mods and Rockers, nostalgia in excess.

I was actually stranded on Jura that night as all the boats had been cancelled due to the high wind. Brilliant! Prior to catching the ferry back to Islay, I took a look at Jura House which was empty and in a mess. The gardens were overgrown and the house neglected. The door was open, so I went inside and picked a few peacock feathers off the floor as a memento of the island. Outside, huge machines in preparation for a private golf course were gouging the land out.

Back on the mainland I went to Stonefield Castle. Not an attraction at all, but a "bespoke hotel" in a stunning location. It was full of Daimlers and Rollers. I took a quick photo and disappeared before the Maître d' moved me on.

I returned back to the Crinnian Canal, which I had previously visited after Kilmartin, as it is a lovely place to spend the night. I spent the day watching sea-going yachts pass through the locks, all fifteen of them. It costs £150 and takes 6-8 hours. The sunset was amazing and I met some modern travellers in the woods, complete with their TVs and heating, all run on generators.

The next day I went for a wonderful walk in Ardcastle Woods near Lochgair and I was stunned by the absolute silence of the place. There was no wind noise and it felt quite bizarre, but it did not last so I moved on to Inveraray. This is a lovely small town, unusual in that all the shop frontages including the supermarkets are black and white. I spent a few hours looking around the prison and museum before driving around Loch Fyne to St Catherine's. On the pebbly beach I found a single red rose and wondered about its history. There had probably been a lover's tiff so the least I could do was rescue the rejected rose.

Despite the torrential rain I went inland to the beauty spot in Glen Croe "Rest and Be Thankful". There was little to see due to the horizontal rain, but the bacon buttie vans were doing a roaring trade, especially with the cold, wet bikers. A group of Japanese bikers stopped nearby and asked me to take their photo. I really admired their positive attitude. Despite the pouring rain, they had travelled all the way up from Manchester. They were still all smiles and happiness, and no British weather grumbles. It was my last night on the mainland before setting off for Bute so I found a lovely spot near the ruins of Clachan Castle. I actually had the van door open as it was relatively warm in the late afternoon. A dog walker got chatting with me and then annoyed me by lecturing me about vaping, so I told him to mind his own business! I think he got the message as he disappeared soon after.

Bute

I did not see Bute at its best due to the mist and rain. Port Bannatyne felt a little run down, but more interesting was St Ninian's Chapel ruins, situated on a promontory which gets cut off at high tide. In the evening I spent a good hour watching the basking seals at Scalspie Sands. There were about twenty pairs, modelling on the rocks in various poses. I passed by "Listening Cottage" which was used during WWII secretly clocking Russian submarines in the loch. On my walk, I met a sweet elderly couple, Pat and Dave, who had met each other just down the road 50 years ago and still happily going strong and jolly together.

Bute Island is generally very green and agricultural, but I have noticed it seems less friendly than the other islands. Unlike on the other Scottish islands they do not wave to anyone passing by. Maybe this is because they get fed up with all the tourists from Glasgow! Mount Stuart is a magnificent gothic mansion inspired by William Burgess and the country home of the Stuart Family. It is also the main reason that people visit Bute. There were a coach load of tourists visiting the gothic mansion, so I gave it a miss and instead watched the video at the Information Centre. It is a very professional and informative film set to ethereal music and artistic videos and there is even a clip of the young Duke swimming naked in his antique pool. Very nice buttocks too!

On the outskirts of the estate, a tiny hamlet with Surrey architecture was built at Kerrycoy for one of the duke's wives who was homesick for the south of England.

Rothesay is a grand Victorian town and the most interesting thing there is its public toilets. You can view the original male urinals (when no men present), built in 1898 by Twyfords. In the evening I watched the big ships come in and out of the harbour. It felt very strange ambling down the promenade as opposed to clambering over bogs.

Back on the Cowal Peninsular, I stayed at a campsite at Kilbride Bay. It was a sandy beach, but too shallow for swimming. The site had several black goats with massive 18in horns wandering about looking quite menacing. Portavadie was my next stop and a surprise. It was all ultra modern with a brand new marina, hotel and spa complex. I met a dog person who informed me she was cooking a birthday cake for her dog. Please treat a dog like a dog, I felt like saying.

Further north, at Otter Ferry, there is a lovely pub called the Oystercatcher. The proprietor agreed for me to say the night in the car park, so I enjoyed a glass of wine in the sunset over the loch and watching the guillemots do their impressive vertical dives. The landlord told me the history of Portavadie. An abandoned oil workers village there cannot be demolished due to the resident protected bats that are difficult to re-house. The new spa complex and leisure centre is being developed by a billionaire who wants to make his stamp (£65billion so far) before he snuffs it. Back at Otter Ferry the next day, I went for a lovely swim and walk around the nearby Ballimore estate - a wooded village of timber houses. Returning to the pub, I had a coffee in the garden and was entertained by the pub dog that ran off with my shoes and Loki's plastic swim chicken.

Venturing inland, I visited Pucks Glen in the Trossachs area, a tiny shady valley full of waterfalls, moss, steps and tiny wooden bridges.

The next bit of my journey was across a beautiful mountain pass from Dunoon to Toward Quay, another end of the road where I had a quiet night.

Back through Dunoon and around Holy Loch I caught my last proper ferry from Hunters Quay across the Firth of Clyde to Ashton on the mainland. I was heading for Largs where I had the luxury of a comfy bed for the night. I stayed with a relative, Eileen, who I had never met before. We had a pleasant time together and caught the boat over to Great Cumbrae Island for the day. The only town, Millport, is a wealthy thriving tourist destination, but not too spoilt. There were dozens of houses for sale and so I joked about radioactivity leaking from the Hunterston nuclear plant opposite. In town there is the narrowest house in Britain, aptly named "The Wedge".

The next day, I briefly stopped at Portencross Castle and Seamill then got stuck on a dual carriageway. It seemed impossible to follow the coast and I kept getting lost or driving around industrial estates. Eventually, I gave up and joined the big road to Troon. I camped by the Royal Troon Golf Club with is palatial clubhouse and walked both ways along the beach. Later I went to the Robbie Burns museum in the picturesque village of Alloway. It is very informative but quite dark in the museum, as all the exhibits need to be protected from the light. As well as being The Bard of Ayreshire, (as I gleaned from the museum) Mr Burns was also a real "Jack the Lad" with the ladies!

Moving south, the next place I stayed was overlooking the pretty village of Dunure with its pub, harbour and derelict castle.

Stopping at Croy Ho, I went for a swim and if I am honest it was the first time in the year that I came out of the sea actually warm. I thought about how the longest day of the year was also approaching and how time flies when you are having fun!

I needed to catch up on my domestics and laundry, so I stayed at the Culzean Country Park camping site. My washing was a disaster as I had overloaded the machine with my sleeping bag and the whole ordeal took over three hours. A visit to Culzean Castle revealed an unusual oval staircase. There was no room to build a round staircase as the castle has restricted space due to being built on a cliff, so both the location and gardens are quite impressive. This site was also used as the location of Lord Summerisle's castle in the film "The Wicker Man".

Along the Road is "Electric Brae", the famous gravity hill. You genuinely appear to be going uphill when, in fact, you are going downhill due to the lay of the surrounding land. This can be proved by putting your car in neutral and watch it "roll uphill" It is an optical illusion and a very powerful one to experience.

I stayed in the harbour at Girvan as I wanted to find out about the magnificent rock plug of Ailsa Craig or Paddy's Milestone as it is called in Ireland. The island is now a bird sanctuary bought recently by the RSPB. However, it does have a "sitting tenant". An Indian business tycoon bought the derelict cottages, but his plans for a hotel were scuttled.

After one night at a Britstop in Ballantrae I went for a pleasant walk on the beach that proved tricky with Loki, as it is a terns nesting ground. Heading for Stranraer the road was getting busy and I was forced to join a convoy of lorries heading for Ireland.

The Rhins of Galloway is a hammer-head peninsular which is where I spent the next few days. I camped at Lady's Bay, very secluded due to tricky access. I had to negotiate deep troughs down a half mile farmer's track. It was worth it though, as it was so peaceful and quiet, my only neighbours being a group of tiny birds swooping and bombing the van in the early evening and following sunrise.

Walking the mile long drive, I arrived at Castle Lochnow which is a private residence with stone eagles on the roof. Scotland's freedom to roam is brilliant for walkers, as well as curious (nosey) people like me. I appreciate this freedom and I think it teaches people to respect the land more. It is the total opposite to England, with its gated communities and private keep out signs.

Portpatrick is a bright and breezy seaside town with an attractive harbour and lots of pubs and guesthouses. The tone of the place was definitely lowered by the "gaggle of girls" in hen gear doing rude things with their dildos, much to the amusement of a group of bikers looking on, but also looking slightly embarrassed. Unfortunately, I fell out with the toilet attendant there. She refused to allow me to fill up my water container. I did it anyway as I was so cross at her jobsworth attitude. Wanting to be on my own again, I stayed near Killantringan Lighthouse.

I was meeting K again, this time on his motorbike, at a nearby campsite. We took a quick drive south to the now clear Mull of Galloway, where we walked the cliffs, saw the homes of thousands of birds and had great views of the Isle of Man and Lake District. Our last night on the north of the Peninsular was one of pure luxury at the beautiful Corsewall Lighthouse Hotel, We chatted over dinner to Evie the waitress, about her Viking brother and paganism. Staying in a lighthouse was the next best thing to staying in a Scottish castle, which I have always wanted to do, but never managed, yet!

At Kirkinner we had an eventful 3-hour walk as we had to make several detours due to a group of frisky bullocks blocking our route. We though that they were testosterone-fuelled and aggressive, but later found out they were hand reared, so they were just after food. Yes we felt a little foolish being scared of peckish boy cows.

Next I got stocked up with books at Wigtown where there is the largest bookshop in Scotland; an amazing den. In fact there are several second hand bookshops there and the town hosts an annual book festival.

Sticking to the coast, we moved on through Kirkcudbright and continued towards Auchencairn. It was very misty, and in the distance we spotted a massive object looming. It was the "Wickerman", standing proudly, arms in the air. I have seen one set alight at the annual music festival a few years ago, and can confirm that it is a daunting sight!

At Kippford we stopped for an ice-cream at the small café and saw the sign "Doggie ice-creams" £1, no joking! This is a small cone decorated with a Bonio instead of a flake. Sadly, we bought one for Loki, a single dog gulp and it was gone. In the sunshine now and we arrived at Sandyhills where there are lots of caves, rock arches and salmon fishing nets in the estuary. It was quite atmospheric on the beach as the mist was all encompassing. We said our goodbyes at Southerness and I carried on to Carsethorne, a small but popular village by the vast expanse of sand, mud and water, ideal for fishermen. The estuary landscape is ever changing, I was really missing my swimming, but I did not fancy quicksand or a mud bath. There is a great pub though called the Steamboat and the old jetty has a memorial for several immigrant families drowned trying to reach America for a better life. It has so many analogies with refugees today fleeing their dangerous homeland and searching for a better life, and being drowned in treacherous waters. Sadly, history repeating itself.

Having skirted the edge of Dumfries to cross the river Nith, my next stop was near Glencapel. A quiet evening was spent watching the birds fishing and a lone man fishing. He was using an old-fashioned "Haaf" net, which were in use hundreds of years ago. They are very large and have a heavy metal frame. You obviously have to be very skilled to use them.

My last but one Scottish visit was at Eastriggs where the "Devil's Porridge" museum is. The munitions factory of WW1 was 9 miles long and produced cordite, a highly toxic and dangerous substance. Thousands of young women worked here putting their lives at risk.

Gretna Green was my last place in Scotland to visit. I had never been before and it was highly unlikely that I would visit for romantic reasons, so I joined the tourists to look at the chapel and blacksmith's Anvil in use since 1754. I did spot a bride and groom, but they were by the side of a busy road. They were not looking very romantic at all.

Well, I was sad to leave Scotland after eight months of beauty and peace. The end of my journey was also looming as it was now July.

July 2015 – Silloth to Longridge

> *"Wherever you go, go with all your heart"*
> **Confucius**

Back in England

On crossing the border I had driving stress, I nearly ended up going up the motorway to Glasgow. Panic! I had to turn around in a "no access" area to avoid it. Positively, I did manage to find the old road that runs parallel to the motorway for about eight miles, with only six cars on it. That was a result and so after a few roundabouts and industrial estates, I began to relax again. The landscape changed to fields scattered with posh villages like Monkhill and Burgh by Sands (no sand), over the salt marshes and following Hadrian's Wall

I eventually arrived at Port Carlisle, a tiny place with characterful houses and one pub. I camped at Kirkland House Farm. I had a field to myself and cold shower which was fine, as the weather had turned hot. I busied myself doing small Bongo repairs and my own simple beauty treatment. The farm owner lent me a book about the area. The village has a fascinating history. At one time an important port with an old railway and canal used many moons ago. A thunderstorm in the night woke me upstairs in the Bongo; lovely as it cleared the air of the mugginess.

Close to Cardurnock I passed by Anthorn radio station overlooking the Solway Firth. It is a NATO facility with

VLF transmitters used for submarine detection. These special transmitters are relatively unaffected by atmospheric nuclear explosions, and consequently used as an early warning system both for the UK and US. The three huge antennas can be seen for miles around and the triangular road patterns around them reflect the remnants of a W.W.1 military airfield. The roads are very windy and hedges high and as a result I kept getting lost and relied upon Brian to navigate me. Even he is not perfect, because if you turn him upside down (like ladies do with maps) he rectifies himself. I find it most annoying.

I went in search of the sea, over more marshes to Skinburness. I found it quite a weird place. Apart from a beautiful but derelict hotel, there is no centre, just bungalows and nowhere to park. The sea was there, but pretty grim and grey.

I stopped next at Silloth which seemed a much friendlier place. It is a port town and due to its attractive cobbled streets and Victorian buildings and pleasant beach it is now a popular holiday destination. The Carrs Victorian flour mill overshadows the town but is still in use today. The promenade is backed with lawns and lots of green areas shaded with pine trees which are all well looked after.

Still in the Solway Firth, but I was desperate for a swim, despite the muddy sea so, to cool down I went for a dip at Maryport. I passed through Flimby, a town dominated by the railway, and the industrial outskirts of Workington. I stopped at a shop for some milk and the woman in the shop assumed I was a camper. I obviously had the wild "coiffure de camping". Maybe I needed to smarten up a bit.

Having nearly got a parking fine at Whitehaven, I looked around the old Haig colliery, which was closed down in 1933. Still standing is the massive chimney called The Candlestick, used to vent methane. Impressively, in the 1980s a flash of lightening ignited the gases for 5 hours. It was possible that without the vent Whitehaven may have exploded.

St Bees Head is an RSPB breeding cliff area. On the walk from a viewing platform, I saw literally thousands of guillemots nesting on the cliff face; a mesmerising site.

St Bees village was really the first place for ages with seaside crowds. There were about 80 people on the big sandy beach. It was good to people watch and see families enjoying themselves together with the odd whingeing child. It is an affluent village with an expensive campsite, so I declined that and moved on to Nethertown. I was able to park overlooking the rock beach and close to a string of shantytown type huts.

Drigg was in my psycho swimming book, so I had to go there. I stayed the night near the beach, which has unusual honeycomb cobble reefs made by worms, and a promise of hearing the Natterjack toad. However, what I really got was a place to stay between an MOD firing range and nuclear dump! The nearby boreholes from Sellafield are known locally as the Drigg suppositories and there are hundreds of them. The nuclear police security came late at night, clocked me, but left me alone and I was awoken early by a group of engineers surveying the nearby field a few feet away. Another borehole, I assume.

The Lake District

I turned left to get some inland beauty for a few days. I travelled up the Wasdale Valley to the head where the road ends at Wasdale Head. WastWater is the deepest lake in England and surprisingly not cold to swim in. It also boasts the smallest church in England, St Olaf, obscured by yew trees.

I went for lots of walks up to the cloud line and passed a few competitive fell running men and cyclists riding up mountains and around the lakes for charity. I prefer to amble around taking in the scenes rather than worrying about time. I was given "unofficial" permission to stay overnight on the village green and the barman at the pub gave me the code to use their camping facilities which was good. The Inn is a great place made up of a maze of stonewalls and stone flags on the floor; good for wet people dripping all over the place. I went in the hill walkers' bar for a cider and felt quite at home. For once my wild and windy look was in keeping with all the other soggy campers. Yes, it was torrential rain that evening.

The following day the weather cleared a little so I managed a walk up the valley before returning to Ravenglass. There I stayed at the C&C site and walked to the old Roman baths in the woods. The village is very old fashioned with flowery cottages along the main street and a small station for the small steam train. Back at camp, as usual, everyone was in bed by 9pm, so I sat outside with only Loki and a friendly toad as company.

The next day I planned to go swimming at Silecroft, a huge sandy beach, but I changed my mind when I discovered that it was covered with hundreds of small purple jellyfish.

From Silecroft I drove through Haverigg crossing four level crossings as the road meanders all over the place. There is a huge prison outside the village of Haverigg and past the marina you come to a collapsed iron ore mine which is now a lagoon. I passed through the holiday village and continued on the rough track around the lagoon. My place for the night was by the old lighthouse built on massive sea defences. It was lovely and quiet and I only saw four people, two cyclists and one horse, that evening.

The following day was beautiful and sunny, so I walked the two miles into Millom. Stopping for a liquid refreshment on the way, I stumbled across a really friendly pub, the Devonshire Arms, in the middle of a housing estate. I wound up the locals about their Christmas raffle and it worked. Several men got their wallets out to buy a raffle ticket and it was there I heard my first Yorkshire phrase "Ay up!" Having helped myself to the hash browns and Loki to the chicken nuggets at the bar, we returned to the van. I had a lovely beach day on the tiny sandy beach. There was one neighbour in a small campervan, Jim was from Earby. I was curious as to whether that was in Lancashire or Yorkshire, so I got a potted history. It is now in Lancashire but previously it had belonged to Yorkshire. The boundaries had been moved in the 70s to avoid Labour votes in certain constituencies; a political ruse.

Barrow on Furness

I drove through the outskirts of the industrial area. Seeing an open top bus, and McDonald's felt a bit like a culture shock. I walked across Sandscale Haws to

Lowsy Point, which is a collection of ram shackled huts with no services at the end of the spit. Very isolated but I did pass a few people along the way who lived there. Then I crossed the bridge onto the Isle of Walney past the huge Trident factory, BEA Systems, which you can see for miles around.

South of the island I walked all around the bird sanctuary and realised that I must have walked most of the deserted beaches that overlook the Barrow offshore wind farm. Vickerstown appeared like a huge modern housing estate and I could not find the centre, so I moved on back over the bridge to Roa Island where the ferry takes you over to Piel Island.

Back on the east mainland coast, I went for a walk along the stony beach at Baycliff. Surprisingly, I found a huge stone inscription there with tributes to Elvis, Bing Crosby, Abba and all the wild swimmers of the 1970s. I found out from a local it was etched by Bill Staples, who died about 15 years ago. He was a nude bather and did not have any time for "grunwicks" (tourists) disturbing his fun.

Piel Island

Returning to Roa Island the next day, there was a crowd at the pier with binoculars and cameras and I wondered what all the excitement was about? A big Swedish ship was being towed across the estuary by a tug boat. It was to be returned to its homeland having failed as a nightclub in Barrow. It took ages to pass and it was going so slowly that it would take three weeks before reaching its Swedish home.

I caught the 11am ferry across to Piel Island. I had a lovely meal at the pub and chatted with the "King of Piel," Steve Chatterway, whilst sipping my wine in the sunshine. He informed me of the customs of the island and how he was crowned as king when he took over ownership of the Ship Inn several years ago. Inside the pub is a large oak chair. If you sit in it you may become a "Knight of Piel" but this will cost you the price of buying a drink for everyone present in the establishment. Back outside I spent the rest of the day swimming and wandering around the 50-acre island and ruined castle. I got so chilled that I fell asleep in the long grass and just missed the last ferry back. The poor ferryman was about to get in his car back at Roa to go home, when he got a phone call. I was Miss Unpopular, but he seemed fine about it. That night I stayed by the bird reserve at Foulney Point. I met the warden who lives one mile out on the spit in a tiny caravan and he proudly told me about his job and love for terns.

I drove on to Ulverston to stock up on shopping and fancied a night in town for a change. It is a lovely town and I spend a good few hours watching five original Laurel & Hardy films in the museum. I treated myself to a pub snack and managed to see a local jazz band. In contrast, the following night it was back to nature, by a railway viaduct on the estuary near Plumpton. That night I went a lovely evening walk and gathered puffballs and samphire.

I noticed the nights were drawing in and realised that the next day was the beginning of the school holidays, so I braced myself for the crowds.

In the morning I moved on to walk around Humphreys Head, by a lovely wild and desolate woodland. Then I was back to civilisation. Grange-over-Sands is really

Grange-over-Grass. I had a look around the twee town full of cafes and B&Bs. Passing the live Sunday morning brass band I walked to the end of the promenade where there is a beautiful derelict lido and at the other end the privately owned Holme Island.

As I had time to spare I went a few miles inland to explore Whitbarrow, a high limestone outcrop with terrific views from the top. The only people about were a group of young rock climbers who left at dusk, so I had a nice quiet night on my own again.

Back on the estuary, I spent some time at Arnside where the tide comes in so rapidly that the coastguard sounds a siren. It is a treacherous channel with deep gullies and quicksand. I picked up a safety leaflet that tells you to lie down spread-eagled if you feel yourself sinking, and whistle! No thanks, think I will just stay off the beach. I did manage to find a lovely spot to camp actually on the beach at Silverdale. I did check the tide timetable and levels to make sure I would not float away in the night.

I drove through Carnforth towards Morecambe and stopped at a laid back site, Red Barnes, as I was in need of a shower. Wandering round by the shore I was surprised to see special tunnel passages in the marshes to allow the elvers (baby eels) to return to the Sargasso Sea! The beach is littered with huge mud boulders where the sea has viciously eaten away at the marches like a ravenous giant.

I was amazed to find out that you can get a double room in Morecambe on the front for £150 a week. I spent a lot of the day attempting to avoid the extortionate £8 a day parking fees. The town appeared a bit run down, but there are some good sculptures scattered around the town. The best one, of course, is of Eric. That night I secured a safe parking place out of town next to a health club. This was a bit of a mistake as I was woken up at 6am by all the pre-work "healthites" arriving for their early morning work out. On my walk, I heard the dulcet sounds of a woman screaming orders to her aerobic class. I am always amazed that people pay money to not only be shouted at, but also be forced to listen to crap pop music! On a more positive note, I passed "Hedwigs House Chicken Sanctuary" for ex-battery hens… sweet.

Heysham is known for its huge power station, but the village nearby is a pleasant surprise. It had wild gardens, flower baskets in bloom and narrow cobbled streets. There is an ancient chapel and 11th Century graves cut into the stone up on the barrow. The people were very friendly and Loki even got two dog biscuits from the smiley road sweeper.

My next port of call was Sutherland Point out on the limb through the marshes and over a tidal causeway. Stopping the van, I spoke to Harold and Sylvia who were parked up the road in a small campervan. They were doing up their 1930s gentleman's yacht in order to turn it into a houseboat. They invited me to stay the night next to them, so I repaid them with several glasses of wine. The next day, I walked all around the headland, through the village and past Sambo's grave. This is a memorial to a young black slave who is thought to have arrived at the port in 1736 with his master. He was taken ill and died at a local inn. It is a poignant reminder of Lancaster's involvement in the slave trade.

In its heyday, this village was the main port for Lancaster and later on a renowned bathing resort. This is no longer the case, as due to changing tides the beach is now a mud flat

I went into Lancaster for information on campsites as I was meeting up with K again in a few days. I ended up going to look at the fantastic mausoleum that looks like St Paul's Cathedral, in Aston Park. Lord Aston had made his money inventing lino flooring and the mausoleum for his wife cost the equivalent of £7 million today. Walking around the park in the sun I discovered that an open-air theatre was performing Oliver Twist that evening. I was determined to see it but all the tickets were sold out. However, I managed to sneak in for free, joining the wandering audience at the second act. The play was superb, good acting and enhanced by the backdrops of the mausoleum dome, woodland and lake side.

Looking for an out of the way place, I went to Cockersands, with its derelict six-sided abbey on desolate and barren land. The first Abbot of the abbey was a hermit, Hugh Garth who was known to have been Master of the Hospital before 1184.The only other unusual fact around here was a sign saying, "No shooting in Lancashire on Christmas Day". This is obviously one of those an ancient laws that is probably still valid today.

The following day, the weather was very wet, so I moved onto Glasson, an official wild camping site by the canal. It was a very social place, despite the rain, full of soggy bikers tucking into their wet butties outside the Travellers Rest café kiosk. Whilst there I met up with wild camping veterans, Jean and Steve from Durham, who had been all over the place in their mobile home. Next to me were Dave and his partner in his green converted ambulance. He invited me in to see his homemade solid oak kitchen units and gypsy style raised bed. He was always on the lookout for other vans to convert. He was making so much money from doing the conversions that he had been able to give up his "proper job". He seemed a clever and resourceful man. I had a lovely dry cosy evening in the van, but the inclement weather continued. Calling at Knott End the following morning I went down to look at the tiny but busy ferry going over to Fleetwood, my next destination.

Driving 20 miles around the Wyre estuary I got to Fleetwood and as the weather cleared, I could see back to Knott end where I had come from. The car park was full of Irish gypsy caravans and a gypsy woman wasted no time in trying to flog me bargain ceramic knives from the boot of her car. Her accent was so broad that I struggled to understand her. I did not buy any knives or fall under her spell for rejecting the offer.

I ended up for the night, on the front esplanade near the Great Euston Hotel at Fleetwood. Here, there was a great view of the whole of Morecambe Bay right up to Barrow on Furness.

As much as I dislike Blackpool, I wanted to put my prejudices away and spend the day here. Much of the town appears very run down and neglected, but I was determined to make the most of my time there. It was cold, windy and rainy, so even the centre of the town was really quiet. I went up Blackpool Tower for the first time and attended the 4pm circus, which provided very good entertainment; good old-fashioned acrobats and trapeze artists with no safety nets. The show went on for two hours, if you included the 30 minutes when they try to sell you all their tat.

I left Blackpool and stayed at Bispham where the promenade and long beach extends through Cleveleys. I swam there, ensuring I did not swallow any seawater, and then went inland again for a few days to camp in a quiet area. I wild camped in the Trough of Bowland watching the gliders play about, picking whimberries and spotting hedgehogs. Beacon Fell is also renowned for its dragonflies or the Devil's Darning needles as they are so called locally. Folklore says that if you fall asleep by the stream they will sew your eyes together.

Later I met up with K and booked in at the local campsite. Unfortunately, this was to be one of the worst campsites of my travels yet. It was ridiculously expensive and the hygiene was atrocious. The club bar was so noisy with multi TVs and kids doing karaoke that one drink was more than enough for both of us.

August 2015 – Chipping to Porth Ceiriad

> *"A ship in harbour is safe - but that is not what ships are for"*
>
> ***John A Shedd***

Chipping was much more pleasant with lots of gentle walks around the old village and traditional pubs. K left and I drove onto Pendleton Moor in search of witches, but there was not even a museum. Returning to the coast via Blackpool, I parked near the pleasure beach to watch the screamers on the Pepsi Max roller caster. At the most southerly end of Blackpool all the hotels were boarded up and it all looks very sad, unlike Lytham, which is a different kettle of fish. The houses overlooking the promenade are all large and detached. There is a large boating lake and a large white windmill. I stayed in the council car park next to the big lifeboat house. The lifeboat is massive as it deals with exceptionally rough seas that can rise over the sea walls at Blackpool. There is also a huge tank-like vehicle that can traverse the extensive sands. The following morning, there were groups of people with rucksacks preparing for the 2-mile hike to reach the sea.

Onwards, and skirting Preston, I managed to find a small road to take me around Hesketh Bank and Banks villages which are set among agricultural fields full of cabbages. It was like Norfolk all over again. I stayed that night at the RSPB reserve on the marshes at Hesketh Out. I spent the next day walking the four miles to Southport. Unfortunately the frontage has been taken over by huge commercial venues and car parks but the town is quite pleasant with Victorian style ornate verandas and coffee places. The mile long pier is the second longest pier in England, after Southend, I assume. By the pier café there was a real crooner singing croony songs in the wind and serenading two elderly dancing ladies.

The next two days were spent at a country campsite a little inland with my friend Elaine from Wales. We had a great time catching up with things and her getting lost and trying to find a pub for a meal. We drove to Crosby to go and see the famous Antony Gormley sculptures. The identical life size iron casts of a naked Mr Gormley were fantastic. A hundred of them stretch for over two miles along the beach and are at various stages of barnacle infestation, dependent on their position. They are stunning, but also quite freaky.

The next day I set off in a hurry and the fridge door flung open dispersing half its contents on the lounge floor and webbed matting, including a carton of cream. After mopping most of it up I found a garden centre that kindly let me use their hose to wash the floor properly. The weather that day was scorching hot so had I not done this I, would have had the smell of a large ripe Camembert in the van for days.

Back at Formby Point Nature Reserve, there were hundreds of people as it was the weekend, but the beach was large enough for them not to be invasive. I made the most of the sun and swam there three times, in the still sandy but cool sea. Loki was so excited to go swimming again, jumping up and down; she even nibbled my bum on the way, which was a bit surprising! In the woods there are old asparagus fields and squirrel feeding platforms. I saw my first red squirrel and there was a group of them performing their acrobatic tricks in the treetops. I stayed the night by the woods as the boy racers were playing in the main car park.

I was dreading driving through the city of Liverpool, so I got there ridiculously early to secure a parking space by the docks. I was so early that nothing was open, so I had to wait two hours before looking around the museum and the Tate.

I took the tunnel to Birkenhead and travelled south as I wished to visit Port Sunlight, the garden village developed by Lord Lever, the 19th Century soap-maker, entrepreneur, philanthropist and humanist. Thirty architects were involved in designing the village complex and every house and private garden is individual. The village had its own school, hospital and swimming pool so it was completely self-contained. The residents working in the soap factory were incredibly well looked after, unique for workers at that time. I bought a slab of bright orange Lifebuoy soap and was on my way.

I kept getting lost in the Wirral for some reason, but made it past Hoylake to West Kirby. I liked this little town with its unspoilt frontage of unpretentious small houses and huge marine lake that everyone walks around. I walked to the three nearby islands over the sands: Little Eye, Big Eye and Hilbre Island. The big one is the only island inhabited part time. I spoke to one of the several lifeguards there who told me that they had had 2,000 visitors there the previous day and I was gobsmacked as only a few dozen were there that day. Mind you, it was blowing a gale, and wet.

I walked along the cliff tops on the Wirral Way footpath looking across the sea to the Great Orme at Llandudno, debating whether to stay the night in England or in Wales. I wanted to enter Wales "through the back door" on the small roads but was foiled at Puddington by a private road. Consequently, I ended up staying at a small mining village on the Marshes called Little Neston with a few houses and small pub. I went for a drink at the pub, the last one of the journey in England and had a wet foot walk along the marshes before settling down in a nice quiet spot for the night. Before crossing the border, I called in at Shotwick down a tiny lane, the last English village before the Welsh border. This place consists only of a few pretty cottages and a church, but there was a man loitering outside his door with his dog. Jack kindly supplied me with water and we chatted about campervans and his art.

Return to Wales

Once over the border, I soon saw the Welsh flags flying. I felt quite emotional, almost like I was arriving home. Through the numbered zones of industrial Deeside big roads were unavoidable. I drove past Shotton Steel works and the power station, and stopped at Flint Castle with its unusual isolated tower. At Llannerch-y-Môr there is an incredible decaying passenger steam ship, the Duke of Lancaster. It was to be a "fun ship" in 1979, but this never happened and it is serving as a canvas for various famous graffiti artists, such as Kiwie.

At the head of the estuary at Talacre Point is a rusty old lighthouse that is slightly skew-whiff. It is a very popular place, but the beach goes on for miles. You have to cross several mud channels to reach the sea. I walked from the crowds to a part where only birds were resting and had a peaceful day in the sun. I could only hear the occasional screams of delight from small children having mud fights. I drove straight through the next stretch of the coast from Prestatyn to Abergele as it is wall to wall caravans parks and cabaret clubs; ideal for families with children, but not for me. At Rhos on Sea, there is the smallest chapel in Wales. It seats six people and is still used for services, but also has a spring with stone steps down to a pool deep enough to baptise an adult.

Travelling over the top of the Little Orme, I was almost blinded by the reflection of the evening sun on the unbroken chain of cars edging the whole front around Llandudno. Not a single space was to be had and it was the busiest town I had been to in the whole of the summer. Llandudno still holds on to its opulence and finesse with all its characterful buildings, the Grand Hotel still looking down over the town like a grand old master. The small Punch & Judy kiosk I saw as a child remains, together with the botanical gardens in the hollow of the Orme. This is Happy Valley where my parents spent their honeymoon many years ago. I paid my £3 toll to go around the Great Orme and drove to the summit. There were fantastic views over Anglesey and a terrific sunset. A very extended family of Indians (about thirty of them and four generations) were enjoying a BBQ and having great difficulty putting out the fire before jumping into their four taxis to return home. I parked in a quiet area near the church for the night. I sat outside the van in the evening from 11pm-2am watching a meteor shower. I saw 75 shooting stars including six beauties with huge trailers arching across the sky.

The following morning, I spotted a group of wild swimmers down a rocky outcrop at Angel Bay. I was tempted to join them, but decided I would finish my journey in one piece instead.

Through Deganwy I took a detour along the Sychant Pass, which was very pretty due to the intense blossom of purple heather. In the valley is a pub call the Fairy Glen and an Austrian restaurant, which I thought was a bit strange. I guess it must be mountain thinking/eating. Skirting Conwy, I arrived at Bangor, where I stocked up on provisions. The weather was so wet and misty I was unable to see much of the town so I made my way over the Menai Bridge to Anglesey.

Anglesey

My first stop was Beaumaris with its castle, small crabbing pier and trendy teashops, but my destination for the night was Penmon Point. The place was quite busy with other vans, fishermen and kids flying kites, but it was also wild and windy and beautiful. It overlooks Puffin Island and has a big black and white lighthouse that rings its bell every 30 seconds. This was quite spooky in the night. I was too late for the puffins, but three dolphins were playing in the sea. I had friends, Ingrid Iris and Pete and my family, my daughter Lisa, Mark and the kids, Lola and Dot visiting over the next few days so I was quite busy entertaining and enjoying myself with them. We stayed in Rhosgoch and went lots of walks and swam in the sea at Cemaes and the hidden Bull Bay.

There are numerous tiny windy roads on Anglesey including those down to Red Wharf Bay and Benllech, with its large sandy beaches. A walk to Point Lynas took me to a lighthouse for sale for a cool million pounds. Port Amlwch has a small harbour and museums informing you about the importance of the area in relation to ships and copper mining and Port Wen has beehive smelters on an isolated beach.

Cemlyn Bay is a miniature Chesil Beach with a freshwater lagoon behind the shore. The north side had a weird imposing fortified house with 20ft high walls. An eccentric military man built it, who not only valued his privacy but the surrounding bird life. I stayed the evening at this beautiful curved bay. I was being checked out at regular intervals, by the armed police patrol connected to Wylfa Power Station and was relieved that they left me in peace.

Inland a little, I explored the ancient village of Din Lligwy near the village of Moelfre. The foundations of the half circle are the best I have seen. Also stunning is Parys Mountain, an extensive copper mine, which dominated the world market in the 1700s. The colours are truly magnificent ranging from copper green to oranges and ochre.

The next three days were wet and horrible, so I did not see much of Church Bay and headed for another Holy Island, the largest one I have visited. All I could see of

Holyhead was a chimney looming in the mist. I ventured into town to a second hand bookshop for my rainy days ahead. I stayed a few miles out of town at the Breakwater Country Park and walked over Holyhead Mountain to North Stack. More impressive is the South Stock with its lighthouse and fabulous views. I managed to get there before the crowds and rain the next day. Courtesy of the RSPB man's binoculars at the Ellis Tower I also saw the last fulmar chick on the island.

Roscolyn is a sandy bay popular with windsurfers and kayakers. A hairy lane gets you there and there are great walks around. I went for a long three-hour walk past St Gwenfaen's healing well traditionally known to cure mental illness, which is most unusual. A dramatic cliff walk takes you past pink cliffs to the white rock arches. The sky was full of low flying jets "playing about". I found out that it was passing out day for the pilots of the local air base. Lots of celebrations or commiserations that night I guess.

Back on Angelsey I stayed at the tiny Cable Bay where, despite the drizzle, I went for an early morning swim. I met Howard and his family who wished me well with my remaining journey and Owen, a sprightly 85 year old beach litter picker.

Just down the road I stumbled across a 2CV 24-hour race practice at the Anglesey circuit. 2CVs were the first vehicular love of my life (sorry Bongo), so I loved watching them bomb around the track and seeing the mechanics tweaking the simplistic engines in the pit stops. After an hour or so, I was bored and left, but only after I had sneaked a "contestants" shower.

The rain continued and so it was yet another "Bongo Day" at Newborough Warren. I had forgotten how persistent and relentless the familiar Welsh drizzle could be. I was getting a bit down in case my last lap of the trip was a washout. I ventured out the next day to do the five-mile walk to magical Llanddwyn Island taking in the extensive dunes, beaches, forests of the pine and pillow lavas on the beach. At the end of the island is an isolated lighthouse and cottages. Llanddwyn means Church of St Dwynwen. She is the Welsh patron saint of Wales equal to St Valentine in England and the island was a shrine in ancient times. Prior to leaving the island, I bought some "posh salt" from Halen Mon, a cottage industry on the straits. I returned to the mainland over the more modern Britannia Bridge heading for Caernarfon.

I parked at the other side of the river for the night overlooking the castle, had a cider at the Anglesey pub then wandered around town. There is a lovely continental feel about the place with its cobbled square and cafes all within the castle walls.

Next, I went inland to Snowdon for a few days as I had time to detour. I drove to the foot of the Cambrian Mountains in the mist. I could not see a thing, all I knew I was going upwards onto the moors near Y-Fron. My ears popped, so I knew I was high up.

I awoke the next morning to panoramic views all over Anglesey. Looking down, I could see how incredibly flat the island was, but I recognised the bumps of Parys Mountains, Holyhead Mountain and Puffin Island. Been there and done them all!

Loki had her photo taken at Bedgellert a popular tourist village where a short walk away there is a brass memorial of the famous dog that allegedly saved a baby and was shot dead due to a misunderstanding. Loki looked as pathetic as ever; "dollop dog" next to the shiny hero dog.

Rhyd Ddu, the toy train station at the foot of Snowdon, was my next night stop. I made it two thirds of the way up the mountain then my knees begged forgiveness. Frustrated at myself for not reaching the top, I spent the evening watching the peak appearing then disappearing regularly in the pink fluffy clouds. It was quite magical.

Returning to the north side of the Llyn Peninsular, I passed Dinas-Delle with its gaudy bright yellow hotel and parked in the rain at the end of the estuary by Caernarfon Airport. Only the dual bladed helicopter and a few private planes were in flight. On the beach, hardy families were attempting to picnic in the blustery wind and rain. This I thought was typical admirable British behaviour.

It was time for another campsite at Gryn Goch. This is a lovely multi-levelled campsite by the beach. I felt quite smug admiring a huge rainbow from the van whilst other campers were frantically re-knocking in their tent pegs in the gales and rain. My luck was in for dinner too, as a mobile pizza van appeared. I even got it delivered across the field and no cooking needed. From the shelter of my van, I watched as some nearby kites frantically had what looked like epileptic fits in the gale.

Despite living in Wales for years, I had not ventured into this beautiful part of Wales. I had a week to spend here before my final arrival at Portmeirion. It proved to be one of my favourite places due to the isolated beaches and wilderness between the villages and towns.

Nant Gwrtheyrn houses the Welsh Language Centre and is at the bottom of a spectacular steep sided valley. The village mining cottages have all been lovingly restored and people now live here again, beautifully surrounded by magnificent quarried mountains.

The next stopover was through Morfa Nefyn in the cliff car park overlooking the tiny village of Porth Dinllaen. This isolated village can only be reached by foot either over the golf course or via the beach. It obviously gets very crowded so I made sure I was up early and walking to the beach before the pub, Ty-Goch, opened. There will be more about that later.

Further down the Western coast, I stayed at the tiny place of Porth Iago. It costs £8 a night to camp as it only had an isolated toilet in a hut by the cliff. However, the location is stunning; the tiny beach is flanked by steep cliffs on both sides. I felt I was back in the Scottish Highlands. I visited more silent whistling sands at Porth Oer and then moved onto the southern headland at Uwchmynydd overlooking Bardsey Island. The drive up the mountain is a tiny steep hairpin type track with few passing places and walking path down also very steep, but panoramic views.

I returned to Porth Dinllaen as they had live music on my last Saturday night. I had a brilliant evening listening to the funky Welsh brass band called Llareggub, which is "Bugger All" spelt backwards, courtesy of Dylan Thomas from "Under Milk Wood". As the evening drew in, so did the tide so people were not only dancing on the beach, but in the sea too. I had a lovely time - my last "wee ha" of the journey.

After one night at Aberdaron I went to Hells Mouth on the south point, famous for its surfers' giant waves. So I got out my blow-up boogie board again and joined them; great fun being battered about. Loki was too scared to enter the sea and just stood at the edge looking all pathetic, like a lost soul and anxious when I disappeared in the swell. I shared a great night with a ruck of young rock climbers from Llanberis - Mark, Tim, Katy, Will and Becky, in their rough and ready transit. Becky got a load of some homemade bobble hats out to sell and sold 3 within 10 minutes. They had just returned from travelling in France and Spain and recommended that I go there next. That is very tempting.

I had only a few days of my trip left, and was feeling very sad at it ending. However, I was proud that I had completed this amazing journey. Heading for Porth Ceiriad, I bonked the rear bumper of the Bongo for the last time on a stone bank on my way to Nant-y-Big campsite. It is located on a cliff top with stunning views across the whole of the Llyn Peninsular as far as Snowdon and Barmouth. It was a breath taking vista as the weather had cleared up. In the distance I could see nearly all the Welsh towns of Cardigan Bay that I had visited at the beginning of my journey.. The owner of the campsite, John, was a jolly sort and proudly told me that they were in the "cool camping" book. I spent that day in and out of the sea and up the down the hills. I was purposely running low on supplies and that evening cooked a very unusual meal. All completely yellow food; scrambled eggs and sweet corn followed by a banana. I felt like one of those weird children who will only eat food of one colour; I was also wearing a yellow dress... mmm.

September 2015 - Borth-y-Gest to Portmeirion

> "Like all travellers, I have seen more than I
> remember and remember more than I have seen"
>
> **Benjamin Disraeli**

It was almost the last day of my travels and so I passed
through Abersoch, which is a bit too trendy for me and

onto the leafy bay of Llanbedrog. It was tricky to follow the coast for a while, ending up at dead ends and lonesome shingle beaches with only seagulls on. I drove on past busy Pwllheli to Criccieth, a pleasant village with more castle ruins, then on to a small road to Morfa Bychan and Black Rock Sands. You can park directly on the beach here, but it is heavily patrolled due to the danger of soft sand. There was no chance of staying the night on the beach as I had planned, as a high spring tide was forecast, which I was disappointed about. Still, I made the most of the day in the dunes, on the beach and in the sea.

Later that day on one of my beach walks I came across my dream house which was for sale for a cool £400,000. The house was called the Powder House and was used as a gunpowder store in WW1. Situated right out on a limb, had it own isolated private beach and land adjoining the golf course, with amazing uninterrupted views across the estuary towards Portmeirion. If only I had the dosh!

Dreaming over, I drove to Borth-y-Gest for my final night by the sea. It is a small village with harbour overlooking the Welsh mountains and Portmeirion Hill. The Mariners Bistro looked inviting and I got all excited choosing my vegetarian snack off the menu as I sat down in the evening sun, outside having a glass of red wine with Loki. I went inside, to order my food and got refused! They only served food with prior bookings, even though I had already secured a table outside. I felt disappointed and quite stroppy, but I let it go as I did not want to spoil my last night. I used my chill mantra, "whatever," and had a cheese and onion toastie in the van instead.

The Journey Ends

Wednesday 2nd September 2015, was my last day of the trip. I went a walk around the nearby woods and small sandy bays interspersed with rocks. I took my last wild swim in one of the tiny beaches and had my last injury, hurting my hand when I slipped on the rocks. I dried off and returned to the Bongo for my last few miles through Porthmadog and over the causeway leading to the village of Portmeirion. Turning right along the lane was where I had turned left 18 months ago. I felt quite emotional, but held it together as I approached the village. There were trucks, cars and crowds of people there, putting up big tops and marquees in preparation for the No.6 festival in a few days. I got all excited as I knew that I would be there celebrating the completion of my trip with my friends. All I needed to do before that was to drop Loki off.

Everyone was busy milling around and it was 2pm when I managed to get a catering lady to take a photo of Billie, Loki and me by the sign in Portmeirion, proof that I had finally arrived at my destination!

There were no trumpets or fanfares but I did send emails to friends and family announcing my arrival saying:-

"Just to let you know, I have arrived…"

(In an electronic voice) *"MY OWN STRING THEORY HAS NOW BECOME REALITY. THE END IS THE BEGINNING."*

Postscript

"Wow, you are brave travelling on your own!" This is what the majority of people I met along the way said to me. I found this quite interesting, especially my own reaction. Initially, but not for long, I felt proud, then it annoyed me as I realised that they would not say that to a man travelling alone. I would then answer defensively (jokingly), "either brave or stupid or mad…" I stopped saying that pretty soon as I knew that it was untrue. I would have preferred they saw me as a spirited, adventurous or even spunky person.

"Gosh, you must have met some really interesting people" was another frequent remark. Well, what is interesting? I think people wanted me to tell them about all these fantasy-like "wow" people who I never met. I certainly did meet some amusing, curious, attractive, interesting and fascinating people. However, I also met some boring and dull ones. All told, I met loads of "ordinary" people, all with their own stories to tell. I did meet many people on the way, and I can say now without any doubt that northerners, i.e. people from Yorkshire and Lancashire, are definitely the friendliest and warmest people in Britain.

"I have always wanted to do that, but I would not do it on my own" or "I have never got round to it" were the other common remarks I got. All I can say is do it when and while you can, but do it in your own way. I only had one dodgy moment due to my initial naivety and I have obviously survived to tell this tale.

Now

Writing this travelogue has been wonderful for me, as I have relived the journey along with the terrific memories of happenings, places and people I met along the way.

Returning to London, I like it less, but am starting to enjoy its variety of accessible fun. Live music, comedy films, all the usual city stuff. I still hate pubs with football blaring out from several screens at a time and having to stand up and shout to be heard. Jura beckons me then!

I cleaned the Bongo and it looks pristine again, apart from the bumper with several lumps out of it which in due course I will rectify. The dashboard, which according to a friend looks like a pagan alter, remains decorated with the relics of my travels.

My Sat Rat, is still standing. He is a small felt rat with no arms and a bongo drum which I bought half way through my journey and which became my travel mascot. The Green Man still is dressed in seaweed and moss and is surrounded by shells of all shapes and sizes including oyster and pebbles, multi coloured seaweed, coral, sea cabbage, heather, sponges. sunflowers and a lot of sand that refuses to leave.

Yes, I miss the sea and have very itchy feet, so am keeping the van. How could I part with it when the trip was the best 18 months - EVER!

Still in the van is the big road atlas of Britain that I used to mark my exact route as I went along with a felt tip pen. Every place I visited has a dot and places I stayed a star. The tatty atlas is now held together with masses of Gaffa tape and it looks like a giant purple slug has crawled haphazardly over all the coastal pages.

What next?

The Bongo is my oyster and I am free to travel wherever I wish!

> *"The sea is calling, I must go"*
>
> ***Pat Heaven***

Abbreviations and Key

Ben	The reluctant part time mobile phone
Billie	The Bongo
Bongo Day	Bad weather day confined to the van
Bongo Fury	A useful Bongo owners club
Brian	Samsung Tablet
Britstop	A great organisation enabling campervans to stay in allocated car parks of pubs, vineyards, farm shops, hotels farms etc. providing that you are polite and support the hosts business.
C&C site	Camping and Caravanning Club (mum and dad) site
Chumpy	Local Welsh saying meaning in a bad mood
Courtney	Mobile Wi-Fi which hardly worked
Devil's Shop	Tesco's
Fair dos	Redistribution of drinks from your friend/neighbours glasses to you own when you have less than them

K	Keith my long term partner
Mushroom roof	A roof that erects sideways as opposed to like a clam as in other Bongos
NT	National Trust
Psycho Swim	Crazy wild swimming equivalent or just dipping
Rough Parking	Wild camping
RSPB	Royal Society Protection Birds
Sat Rat	My lucky dashboard mascot
Slap down meal	Cheap and cheerful meal
White Fridge	Big motor home
Winston	My invaluable Pills beatbox for music played through Brian
Photographs	Send an email to **blogoff@f2s.com** for link to Flickr.

Acknowledgements

A big thank you to:

Keith - who in his own words "chased me around the country" supplying me with invaluable OS maps, vaping equipment and contact lenses. He also helped with the publishing and has supported me throughout.

Lana - for typing up the manuscript.

Iris and Peter – for proof reading.

Hosts and Visitors along the way:

Elaine, Lisa and Mark, Lola and Dot, Luke and Louise, Roger, Tina and Pigiron, Vic and Aide, Ellie, Anje, Iris and Peter, Ingrid, Kath and Ian, Ray and Sue, Eileen.

Caroline – for the hospitality at her home near St Ives.

Claire and Ricardo - for sharing their flat at Rattray Head

Emma and Ian - for the cheese and wine evening at Durness.

Sarah and Martin for their generosity and Bongo sitting at their house at Dunnet.

Last but not least:

Loki dog - for being my best friend and coolest travelling companion ever.

About the author

Pat has been many things in her life: potato sorter, garage pump attendant, hospice nursing assistant, carer, barmaid, shop assistant, potter and pottery teacher. She finished work as a qualified mental health nurse and therapist in 2014.

She is originally from Stockport, has lived many years in Mid Wales and now resides in London with her partner.

She has two daughters and four granddaughters.

23579441R00139

Printed in Great Britain
by Amazon